The Activated Church

The Activated Church

How to Tap
the Awesome Potential
of the Local Church

By Dr. Karl A. Barden

Unity Library & Archives
1901 NW Blue Parkway
Unity Village, MO 64065

07/09

Destiny Image Publishers
P.O. Box 310
Shippensburg, PA 17257-0310

"Speaking to the Purposes of God for this Generation"

ISBN 1-56043-067-2

For Worldwide Distribution
Printed in the U.S.A.

Contents

Preface

To truly know Jesus Christ is to have received practical living revelation of servanthood and of Christ *the* Servant of all. "Behold! My Servant," Isaiah says of Him (Isa. 42:1). Jesus testifies of Himself, "I am among you as the One who serves" (Luke 22:27).

Unfortunately, in reality servants with a true understanding of servanthood are in short supply in the contemporary church.

Servanthood—especially that which is inconvenient or costly—has been lost as a mandatory concept of Christianity. With today's attraction for "power" ministry and "public" ministry, few feel drawn to the servanthood life. Those who do much serving too often see it from the perspective of "what I can do for God" or as a step toward personal promotion.

Servanthood is a revelation of Christ that the Church of Christ today desperately needs. This book is written as a call to Christians everywhere to hear the word of the Lord regarding servanthood and to respond obediently. It also provides practical, how-to instructions for beginning a life of servanthood for each and every member of the local church.

In these last days, it is said, God is raising up a many-membered body, a manifested son, a remnant, a manchild, an overcomer. What will he be like? The answer will surprise you. The New Testament Book of Revelation is written exclusively to those identified as "His servants" (Rev. 1:1; 22:6). It is "servants" who are sealed on their foreheads with the name of Christ and God (Rev. 7:3; 14:1). After the Gospels, the Book of Revelation uses the words "servant," "servants," "serve" and "service" more times than any other writing of the New Testament.

Have we missed the message of the last book of the New Testament because we did not qualify as the "servants" to whom it is addressed? The most crucial of end-time messages turns out to be the most practical. With the Christian masses of the Church having their eyes on the Middle East and on all the fanciful speculations of what should happen next, they have forgotten the mandate to attend to themselves in order to be spotless, unblemished expressers of the life and service of Christ. That the Church may wake up and receive this vital end-time revelation of servanthood is my deeply felt prayer.

Karl A. Barden, D.D.S., D. Min., 1991

Further Study for Personal Enrichment

Preface

1. To truly know Jesus Christ is to have received practical living revelation of _____ and of Christ *the* _____ of all.

2. Servanthood—especially that which is inconvenient or costly—has been lost as a _____ concept of Christianity.

3. To whom is the Book of Revelation exclusively written?

Chapter One

Commission to Serve

Then to Adam He said, "Because you have heeded the voice of your wife, and have eaten from the tree of which I commanded you, saying, 'You shall not eat of it': Cursed is the ground for your sake; in toil you shall eat of it all the days of your life. Both thorns and thistles it shall bring forth for you, and you shall eat the herb of the field. In the sweat of your face you shall eat bread till you return to the ground, for out of it you were taken; for dust you are, and to dust you shall return."

Genesis 3:17-19

What a tragedy...the way we Christians have read and understood this scripture! Most or us suppose it to be the beginning of the history of man and work. One word says it all: cursed. We have believed that parched ground, thistles and sweat represent the required punishment, toil and travail each person is destined to endure daily. We have used this scripture to believe, and therefore fulfill, that work is the curse Adam brought upon his entire race. We think that since Adam fell and was cursed with work, we, his fallen descendants, are miserable victims of the same evil. Consequently, we commonly view pre-fall

1

Adam as a truly free spirit, without care, serene and on eternal holiday with God. How we long to return somehow to that state! It all seems very unfair.

Both ideas are grievous deceptions and misreadings of the Bible. It is wrong thinking to consider work as part of the curse; it is just as wrong to think that Adam did not labor before he sinned. Before there ever was a curse to pronounce, God created His man and His woman for a purpose that is glorious, endless and pleasing to Him. That purpose is *work*. Indeed, that purpose is *service*.

> *Then the* LORD *God took the man and put him in the garden of Eden to tend and keep it.*
>
> Genesis 2:15

Man is created to work and to serve. Work is an integral and inseparable function; it is united to man's physical being. He was created with a body and with strength. He has a heart, soul and spirit. He has a mind with the capacity to understand, know, reason, feel and decide. He has abilities, skills, talents and a drive for life. All of these endowments are designed by his Creator as areas through which he may work and serve.

When God finished each aspect of His creation, He declared, "It is good." Over all of it He declared again, "It is very good." God made both pronouncements over the man and, by extension, over the man's purpose. In other words, when God said, "Very good," the connected ideas of man, work and service were included.

Man is commanded to work and to serve. In His first recorded words to man, God commissioned him to undertake a responsibility.

Then God blessed them, and God said to them, "Be fruit-ful and multiply; fill the earth and subdue it; have dominion over the fish of the sea, over the birds of the air, and over every living thing that moves on the earth."

Genesis 1:28

Thus, man's service is always to God first; it is the created to the Creator, the servant to the one Master. Man does not labor because he is hired, but, by virtue of birth, to fulfill his created purpose. *Service and work are the fundamental means by which man can obey God.*

Today's *man is obliged to work and to serve.* He is obliged because he is owned by his Creator and because he is bought by the blood of his Redeemer. He does not own himself. There is no room for self-service in God's plan for man.

Or do you not know that your body is the temple of the Holy Spirit who is in you, whom you have from God, and you are not your own? For you were bought at a price; therefore glorify God in your body and in your spirit, which are God's.

I Corinthians 6:19-20

This is a radical message for a world devoted to caring, serving and gratifying self. Most people today are simply unaware of the concept of serving Christ, His Body or their fellowman. "Look out for number one" is the current philosophy.

In sharp contrast, sincere appreciation of God's ownership brings realization of God as "number one." This truth sets men free from bondage to self.

Man is blessed and privileged to work and to serve. The proverb of the medieval trade guilds was "Work is worship." Service is another word for worship. In Romans 12,

3

Paul urges believers to present even their bodies sacrificially to God in worshipful service. Of course, by "bodies" he means the whole physical capacity to do or to work. This, Paul goes on to say, is only reasonable. It is possible to know through daily experience the reasonableness and blessedness of work. Rather than being oppressive drudgery, work and service are to be a full and free expression of gratitude, love, delight and adoration for the Lord. When we work as God always intended us to work, we are blessed.

Man is created to work and to serve. He is commanded, obliged and privileged to work and to serve. In the face of these facts, how wrong is the prevailing thought that service, or work, is a curse! We are taught by the times to live for the three-day weekend and to demand a shorter working week. We Americans spend enough money on recreation, sports and leisure to feed and clothe the rest of the planet.

The thought "work equals curse" leads directly to resistance and opposition to God's plan. It causes people to curse what God has blessed; and so they become self-created victims. Their attitude makes it so. The truth is, there is *no more curse*; Christ died and redeemed mankind. Christ has effectively removed any excuse for disdaining or avoiding service and work.

But where God requires, God leads. He has demonstrated His own giving and service in love. He served with the greatest service possible by committing the life of His own Son as an offering for sin, thus restoring fallen man to relationship and to fellowship with Himself.

> *For God so loved the world that He gave His only begotten Son, that whoever believes in Him should not perish but have everlasting life.*
>
> John 3:16

Moreover, God, manifest in flesh, became the servant of all in order to reveal the path of service we are to follow. Because Christ as a man could be a servant to all, all men can serve. Indeed, all are to model themselves after Christ, the Pattern. Christianity is service; Christianity is work. All Bible passages about "entering His rest" are meaningless if Christianity is not work. Rest presupposes prior service and work. The very promise Jesus made of light yoke and easy burden admits, nonetheless, the requirement of burden and yoke. Where there is no visible expression of servanthood there is no visible expression of Christianity. It is impossible to have Christianity without service.

> *The Son of Man did not come to be served, but to serve, and to give His life a ransom for many.*
>
> Matthew 20:28

> *For who is greater, he who sits at the table, or he who serves? Is it not he who sits at the table? Yet I am among you as the One who serves.*
>
> Luke 22:27

> *So when He had washed their feet, taken His garments, and sat down again, He said to them, "Do you know what I have done to you? You call me Teacher and Lord, and you say well, for so I am. If I then, your Lord and Teacher, have washed your feet, you also ought to wash one another's feet. For I have given you an example, that you should do as I have done to you. Most assuredly, I say to you, a servant is not greater than his master; nor is he who is sent greater than he who sent him."*
>
> John 13:12-16

In a day when comfortable circumstances, increased health and wealth and public popularity are thought to be signs of divinely sanctioned Christianity (thus reflecting in measure our erroneous mental picture of unfallen Adam), the desperate, crucial need of the Church is to learn to bow her knee to Christ the *Lord* in obedient, adoring service. The tragedy is that, for the most part, she either ignores or is ignorant of her need.

To present both the need and the solution is my purpose for writing. My desire is that in the following chapters, you will find an increased biblical understanding of service, discover your own role as a servant of Christ and most importantly, receive personally the heart of genuine servanthood. "Oh, to be like Jesus" voices the deep longing of every true believer. Servanthood is God's answer and our means of true fulfillment.

Further Study for Personal Enrichment

Chapter One

1. In a sentence, describe how we usually view pre-fall Adam.

2. Identify God's glorious, endless purpose in creating man and woman.

3. Cite two things that oblige a man to work and to serve His Creator.

4. Why is service a radical message to today's world?

5. If work and service to the Lord are not to be oppressive drudgery, what are they to be?

6. Man is created to work and serve. He is _____ , _____ and _____ to work and serve.

7. Where does the thought "work equals curse" lead?

8. Christ has effectively removed any _____ for disdaining or avoiding service and work.

9. What is needed for a visible expression of Christianity?

10. Cite the desperate, crucial need of the Church today.

11. In a paragraph, express which concepts were new to you or which challenged you as you studied Chapter One.

Chapter Two

Wanted: Joy, Security and Freedom

Everywhere across the land I have observed church buildings occupied by souls whom I call "poor, miserable Christians." They are disheartened, discouraged, disappointed, lackluster and dismal. They see themselves as spiritually penniless and powerless. Christianity has lost its initial excitement and glitter for them. They have settled down to live a life of religious subsistence—observance of rules and policies and involvement in services and programs which they feel are required. They are unhappy—contagiously unhappy—victims of a religious, legalistic system they think is Christianity.

Poor, miserable Christians are characterized by a key trait: They are tired. They become tired because they are fighting God. He, by His Spirit, is eternally working to lead them out of misery and into a lifestyle of true Christian joy, security and freedom. All the while they resist, clinging steadfastly to the measure of false security they have received from sub-standard Christian living.

Perhaps I am describing you. Perhaps you are asking yourself, "Where has all the joy gone?" Beneath your pretenses you can admit to feelings of discontent, insecurity or misery. You are tired. You have honestly wondered if your current lifestyle is all Christianity has to offer.

I would like to show you a different and better way of living. It is possible to reenter the joy of the Lord. It is possible to have security in Jesus. It is possible to end misery and resistance to God and His people. It is possible to truly know all of the promised positive aspects of Christianity that God has to offer. True Christian joy, security and freedom are found and developed in the experience of serving in His Kingdom, the Church.

JOY

Many Christians define joy as the way they wish they were living. They believe it to be a self-determined, comfortable combination of service to self, to the world and to God. To them, joy means "I get what I want, when I want, under the conditions I want and in the proportions I want." In other words, they think that "I want" plus "I get" equals joy.

I do not suppose that anyone really believes this philosophy when it is stated like that. But Jeremiah was right when he wrote that "the heart is deceitful above all things, and desperately wicked" (Jer. 17:9). In this matter of joy being associated with material gain—the classic dogma of health, wealth and happiness—how swiftly does the Church deceive herself! Christians willingly try to capture immediate pleasure by adopting the false idea that gain demonstrates godliness. "After all," they inwardly reason, "if we do whatever we please (that which is right in our own eyes) and can get whatever we please, then we are able to determine and attain a level of happiness for ourselves. 'All work and no play makes Jack a dull Christian.' "

Temporal gain, of course, cannot bring lasting joy. In fact, the more one owns, the more opportunity one has for things to go wrong. If anything, pursuit of temporal gain represents enjoyment of "the passing pleasures of sin" (Heb. 11:25). Pursuit of joy through the practice of "I want" plus "I get" does have its emotionally satisfying moments, but eventually it produces for the poor, miserable Christian even longer-lasting feelings of guilt and misery.

In his *American Dictionary of the English Language* of 1828, Noah Webster defines "joy" as the "passion or emotion excited by the acquisition or expectation of good; that excitement of pleasurable feelings which is caused by success, good fortune, the gratification of desire or something good possessed, or by a rational prospect of possessing what we love or desire."

True and lasting joy is indeed an emotion. It is a delight of the mind based on present or future good. It is the experience of pleasant peace or serenity of the conscience. Joy is also a fruit of the Spirit, according to Galatians 5:22. Therefore, joy is a character trait of an authentic Christian.

Joy is marked by the following emotions and expressions:
1) satisfaction, because desires are accomplished;
2) contentment, through enjoyment or celebration of possessions, whether or not temporal;
3) triumph, in overcoming opposition;

4) gladness—joy in moderation;

5) exultation—joy in the extreme; and

6) cheerfulness—the regular attitude of joy.

Joy is an emotion, expectation and gratification. But none of these require joy to be either an enduring emotion or a fruit of the Spirit. If joy is to be an eternal characteristic and pleasure of the believer, then all his feelings, expectations and gratifications must be focused on and derived from eternal things. The joy *of the Lord* is your strength (Neh. 8:10).

Hypocrites do not have lasting joy. They are sad. They are miserable. They suppose that practicing Christian disciplines must include unfair pain and distress. Jesus warned:

When you fast, do not be like the hypocrites, with a sad countenance. For they disfigure their faces that they may appear to men to be fasting. Assuredly, I say to you, they have their reward. But you, when you fast, anoint your head and wash your face, so that you do not appear to men to be fasting, but to your Father who is in the secret place; and your Father who sees in secret will reward you openly.

Matthew 6:16-18

Hypocrites are not the lost; they are the religious people who are without joy. Jesus clearly shows the contrast between the sad hypocrites and those whose countenances appear anointed, washed and clean, even shining. Their secret relationship with their Father is evidenced by open reward. Nonetheless, their relationship with their Father is reward enough.

How is lasting joy to be attained? How is it to be received? The parable of the talents answers by showing that joy is the reward for faithfulness *in service*.

> *After a long time the lord of those servants came and settled accounts with them. So he who had received five talents came and brought five other talents, saying, "Lord, you delivered to me five talents; look, I have gained five more talents besides them." His lord said to him, "Well done, good and faithful servant; you were faithful over a few things, I will make you ruler over many things: <u>enter into the joy of your lord.</u>" He also who had received two talents came and said, "Lord, you delivered to me two talents; look, I have gained two more talents besides them." His lord said to him, "Well done, good and faithful servant; you have been faithful over a few things, I will make you ruler over many things. Enter into the joy of your lord."*
>
> Matthew 25:14-23 (Emphasis added.)

As the parable continues, Jesus explains that the servant who is not faithful to his God-given commission and ability is punished for faithlessness. Jesus' emphasis on the third servant, however, does not mean that the promotion of the two faithful servants should go unnoticed. On the contrary, five key elements of their faithful service are worthy of specific mention.

1. We serve according to our natural abilities. God does not call on us as Christians to be something we are not. He does require that we use what we have. What is our personality? What are our strengths and weaknesses? What are our mental capabilities? What knowledge do we already possess? What skills do we have? He reviews our abilities before He ever assigns a task to us. In the same way the Bible promises we will not be tempted beyond our present ability to withstand (I Cor. 10:13), neither will He require us to serve above or below our "several abilities."

2. We serve according to His commission and endowment. When God assigns a task, He invests us with all the necessary and appropriate spiritual gifts and resources in order for the job to be accomplished, and correctly. He does not intend that either the job or we should fail. He commissions us for our success and possible subsequent promotion. Accordingly, He bestows His divine graces for our use and multiplication. Complaint is never due; He does not leave us short-handed or without the necessary spiritual capabilities. All of Christ's provisions are available for our use. We are seated together with Him, enthroned in the highest heavens (Eph. 1:3; 19-23; 2:5-7). From the vantage point of His throne (thus our throne), we are to carry forth His directives.

3. We are to serve faithfully. Faithfulness is an important feature of the master's commendation. "Well done, good and faithful servant." God appoints us for the faithful achievement of reasonable daily duties. It is *reasonable* service that He requires (Rom. 12:1). Great, spectacular or consequential worldly success and worldly joy do not receive God's smile, or even His recognition. God recognizes, honors and promotes diligent, steady, faithful, day-by-day service.

4. Our needs are already met. We receive provision for our needs when we open our spiritual eyes and recognize our places as God's servants. All our cares and needs are daily provided for from our Master's stores because we are intimate members of His own household. Too many Christians do not see themselves as servants fully cared for by their Owner-Master. They view their relationship to the Lord as one of a hired employee. They work to earn the Master's wage from which they must provide for their daily needs.

Present American economic practices seem to contribute highly to present American Christian spiritual perspectives. We are taught to think and behave from a position of lack. Modern advertising advances this position as her sole crusade. She incessantly sounds the clarion of dissatisfaction—with everything. In her temple of the printed page and of the broadcast word she daily teaches us to believe we always have a need for more. As a result, many Christians think spiritual maturity involves progressive accumulation of material blessing. Instead, maturity involves progressive realization and use of what the Lord has provided already. Martin Luther has noted truly that the Lord "quite often gives riches to those from whom he withholds spiritual good."[1]

In all our dealings before God and toward one another we are to function from the place of fullness, never from lack. Truly free people are those who profoundly know and believe that all their needs are overseen and supplied in abundance by a loving, caring God. From an attitude of abundance they lavish abundance, freely distributing many graces of Christ's atonement on those who will

---

1.   Scheidt, David L. ed., *Martin Luther's Table Talk* "Wealth Is Nothing," The World Publishing Company, Cleveland, 1969 (First Printing).

receive. Since they freely received, they freely give. They are enabled to not be anxious for the things "that the Gentiles seek," for they believe their heavenly Father knows and sees their needs. They are truly free to seek first the Kingdom of God for themselves and others (Matt. 6:31-33).

5. Spiritual promotion results from natural faithfulness. When Paul says, "However, the spiritual is not first, but the natural, and afterward the spiritual" (I Cor. 15:46), he refers to physical resurrection. He compares Adam's created body of earth to Christ's resurrected body from heaven. However, this scripture is often used to illustrate a different issue. By saying, "First the natural, then the spiritual," we mean that natural responsibilities develop and prove spiritual characteristics. Nowhere is this principle illustrated more clearly than in Jesus' concluding remarks in another story about servanthood—the parable of the unjust steward. In this parable, Jesus teaches that Christian servants must be found faithful in three areas in the natural in order to receive spiritual privileges and responsibilities.

> *He who is faithful in what is least is faithful also in much; and he who is unjust in what is least is unjust also in much. Therefore if you have not been faithful in the unrighteous mammon, who will commit to your trust the true riches? And if you have not been faithful in what is another man's, who will give you what is your own?*

> Luke 16:10-12

First, a Christian servant must be proven faithful "in that which is least," or in little things. Genuine servanthood is demonstrated by one's paying attention to the smallest details even when not observed by others. Little foxes spoil the vines of progress to maturity and servant-hood. Conversely, the spiritual reward for proven faith-fulness in this natural area is "much," or great spiritual responsibility.

Second, a Christian servant must be proven faithful in "the unrighteous mammon," or in money matters. Un-righteous money must be handled righteously, put to good use for the Kingdom and not to illegitimate use for self. Selfish drive for money is motivation that stems from a position of lack. It is rebellious disbelief in God's will-ingness to provide for and suitably advance His servants' lives. On the other hand, proven faithfulness in money matters releases the promise of "true riches," the realized superabundance of the (spiritual) wealth of Christ.

Third, a Christian servant must be proven faithful in "that which is another man's," or in matters entrusted to him by another. So speaking to leaders, is not the care and oversight of the leader's own family a sacred trust that has been received from the Lord? When a pastor's own home is in order, he demonstrates his faithfulness in what belongs to another, meaning the Lord Himself. According to First Timothy 3:5, it is on the condition of this faithfulness that greater responsibility can then be entrusted. The spiritual promise for being proven faithful in what has been entrusted is in "that which is your own." "That which is your own" I believe to be a Christian maturity of character that carries its own inherent and compelling authority.

The connection between servanthood and joy also is made in the parable of the hidden treasure.

*Again, the kingdom of heaven is like treasure hidden in a
field, which a man found and hid; and for joy over it he
goes and sells all that he has and buys that field.*

                                                  Matthew 13:44

The Kingdom of heaven, the field, is the Church. The
treasure is the glories, virtues, excellencies and godly attributes of her people. Her owner is Christ. Everyone who
may discover and desire her treasure must "sell all" and
"buy into" her. To "sell all" is to relinquish the entire investment—the whole of life—for the sake of gaining the
field, especially its treasure (but also including its imper-
fections). Further, no one buys a field simply to look at it,
or it would soon go to weeds. A field is bought to be
worked, to produce a harvest. In a very real sense, the
owner serves the land by his working the field. Ownership does not produce a harvest (of joy); work or serving
produces the harvest.

For believers who would be servants, practical expression of "selling all" is full and final renunciation of sin,
and then of self. Renunciation of self includes the aban-
donment of personal rights—the individuality, time,
money, property, knowledge, efforts and skills which we
previously held as our own. All these are under God's
ownership; therefore, they are submitted to His control.

"Selling all" is denying self, taking up our cross daily
and following Jesus. The parable teaches that joy comes
from selling all for the sake of the field. In selling all the
buyer gives the field and its treasure priority over all his
goods.

The irony is that, when you truly sell all to buy, or
"buy into," the field and its treasure, the field and its

Owner buy you. Jesus teaches that "where your treasure is, there your heart will be also" (Matt. 6:21). He is calling for an exchange of treasures. I exchange my treasure—my so-called rights of individuality, time, money, property, knowledge, efforts, skills and so forth—for His eternal treasure hidden in His Church. In the process, His Church becomes all my joy.

"Enter the joy of the Lord" is both a command and an opportunity. But fulfillment depends on the servant. The entry into joy is through service and servanthood.

SECURITY

According to Webster (1828 edition), "security" means "protection; effectual defense or safety from danger of any kind." It is "freedom from fear or apprehension; confidence of safety." Insecurity is a lack of safety or a lack of confidence in safety; it is uncertainty, danger, hazard or exposure to destruction or loss.

From a purely natural perspective, the idea of "selling all" is more conducive to insecurity than to security. As so frequently happens, the biblical presentation of truth is diametrically opposed to the world's presentation. "Selling all" brings true security. Withholding results in insecurity.

> Do not fear, little flock, for it is your Father's good pleasure to give you the kingdom. Sell what you have and give alms; provide yourselves money bags which do not grow old, a treasure in the heavens that does not fail, where no thief approaches nor moth destroys. For where your treasure is, there your heart will be also.
>
> Luke 12:32-34

"Selling" what you have and investing in heavenly treasure is the theme of this scripture. Surrounding this theme are two important facts. First, the will and pleasure of the Father is to present His Kingdom. If you will sell, He will give. Second, where you "sell" or invest your substance is where you invest your heart. The more you sell yourself and your substance to the Father's pleasure— His Kingdom, the Church—the more your heart will be in the Church. The more your heart is in the Church, the more security you have. You are secure because you know assuredly in what kingdom your heart lies.

 Those who are truly members in a local church have invested themselves—all that they are and all that they have. They are totally secure because of the high price they paid. They deposited themselves. They deposited themselves in the Church. That means they deposited themselves in the lives of people of that local church. It is difficult, if not impossible, to criticize someone in whom you have deposited yourself, made an investment of your love, your care, your ministry. One of the great self-tests for a critical spirit is to ask yourself these questions: "Am I grateful for those toward whom I am frustrated?" "Am I investing in them?" "Am I praying for them?"

In our own congregation, our catechism ministry is perhaps the single most important program for solidly establishing believers in Christian understanding and experience. Catechism works. It is not because of the quality of doctrine that is printed and preached, although that is essential. Catechism works because of the "Catechism Counselors" assigned to all students.

Weekly home study lessons call for objective and especially subjective answers, so catechism students share their souls as they regularly write about their growing relationship with the Lord. But in response to the students' own words and on every student's paper, the Catechism Counselors themselves write words—words of ministry. They write words that are personal, relational and real; words of praise and encouragement; words of care, commitment and prayer; and words of individual identification with the students' own experiences. The ministry in writing to each individual is substantial.

But ministry does not stop there. Counselors and students share snacks and often meals together. They socialize and play together. They pray together. They study together. All this is on a regular, if not weekly, basis.

From years of experience we have proven that it is this quality of ministry investment that is needed for establishing unshakable Christians for Christ. Catechism works because investment in one-on-one ministry works.

Security comes from being joined to a body where this sort of investment between members can freely take place. Even the word "member" means "joined appendage." A member is a limb—a leg, arm, ear, finger—that is a subordinate part of the main body. A member is secure because of its specific function in relation to the whole body. The whole body is secure because of the proper functioning of each of the various parts. But membership also includes obligations of function or of responsibility.

For even when we were with you, we commanded you this: If anyone will not work, neither shall he eat. For we hear that there are some who walk among you in a

21

disorderly manner, not working at all, but are busybodies. Now those who are such we command and exhort through our Lord Jesus Christ that they work in quietness and eat their own bread. But as for you, brethren, do not grow weary in doing good.

II Thessalonians 3:10-13

In this instance Paul refers to the membership obligation of work or service. Work, or service, is a membership requirement of the local church. It is a sign of joining. It is a sign of security. "If you do not work then you should not eat" is another way of saying that no privileges are allowed without the fulfillment of necessary responsibilities. That is a universal principle. It applies for the labor force and for the servants in the local church. It is both a natural and a spiritual principle. In the natural, the person who refuses to work soon starves, at least where there is no welfare assistance. In the spiritual, the person who refuses to be joined to the Church via service and a servant's heart soon weakens and withers spiritually. His status as "eternally secure" is called into question, for if his fruit bearing stops, the Father may prune him from the vine and cast him into the fire.

As far as the obligation for work or service is concerned, no distinction is made between natural and spiritual. We believe and practice this in our own local church. One of the most "spiritual" areas of service in our church is the Custodial Crew. Most people would consider it one of the most natural of crews. Yet, it is one of the most popular of all the opportunities to serve. On Custodial Crew, fathers who work beside their young children train them in the skills of natural care and maintenance as well as the heart of a servant. On Custodial Crew, college students and new church members often get their first taste of local church community life, including a sense of value, importance, camaraderie and *esprit de corps.*

Each of our service crews has a service manual for its members. The "Introduction to Custodial Crew" profoundly illustrates the principles we have been discussing. It reads as follows:

Vision

But you shall appoint the Levites over the tabernacle of the Testimony, over all its furnishings, and over all things that belong to it; they shall carry the tabernacle and all its furnishings; they shall attend to it.

Numbers 1:50 (KJV)

Purpose

The purpose of the Living Faith Fellowship Custodial Crew is to minister to the Lord Jesus Christ by developing a servant's heart within each crew member, nurturing close, interpersonal relationships between crew members and maintaining thorough cleanliness of the church building.

Goals

God holds a great concern for the proper care of His house of worship, so much so that at the establishment of the tabernacle of Moses, He ordained a special people, the Levites, to maintain and care for that facility. Your duties as part of the Custodial Crew of Living Faith Fellowship—modern day equivalent of the Levitical servants—likewise are held in high regard by our Lord. And He delights in the example set here as we present His house to the world, in order and (desirably) "without spot."

We call this the <u>Custodial Crew</u> for a reason. We do not do a janitorial service. "Janitor" too often carries the sense of just doing a job. Rather, we have been given the service of keeping custody of this facility, a possession of our Lord which requires the highest degree of stewardship.

The cleanliness of this building is often the first impression a person receives of Living Faith Fellowship. Hence, custodial service does not end after Saturday or Tuesday crews. We are always keeping an eye on the facility to make sure that it is exhibiting excellence in appearance. Our heart is to serve Jesus by making sure that His building is as clean as possible. If there has been dirt tracked into the building, chances are a custodian will notice and clean it up. If a restroom has been left messy, a custodian will not stand by and let it remain so.

Serving God in this manner, we strive to 1) develop a servant's heart in each crew member; 2) develop close, interpersonal relationships within the crew; 3) recognize and develop leadership potential; 4) train each crew member in new skills; and 5) complete our job thoroughly and efficiently. Additionally, our service releases our pastors to more effectively seek God and His Word and minister to the Body.

As you enter into this service, you are part of the overall Living Faith Fellowship team, working in unity to effectively minister to the Lord Jesus Christ, to the Church, to the community and to the world.

Manuals for all of our service crews contain similar vision and goal statements, as well as job descriptions and other necessary information, policies and procedures. Fundamentally they all put forth the vision that natural work is spiritual. No distinction is possible. All work is "unto the Lord."

> *Bondservants, be obedient to those who are your masters according to the flesh, with fear and trembling, in sincerity of heart, as to Christ; not with eyeservice, as menpleasers, but as bondservants of Christ, doing the will of God from the heart, with goodwill doing service, as to the Lord, and not to men.*
>
> Ephesians 6:5-7

> *And whatever you do, do it heartily, as to the Lord and not to men, knowing that from the Lord you will receive the reward of the inheritance; for you serve the Lord Christ.*
>
> Colossians 3:23-24

The first responsibility as mentioned in every job description in every service manual carries the same message: Service to the Lord Jesus is the premier goal of all work that is done. Examples are the following two descriptions from the Custodial Crew manual:

> The Custodial Crew Leader must have a close personal relationship with our Lord Jesus Christ and a God-given desire to serve Jesus and His Body.

> The Custodial Crew member should be growing in a vital relationship with our Lord Jesus Christ and exercising a servant's heart.

To reiterate, security and servanthood encompass these points:

1) Servanthood is work.

2) All work is spiritual.

3) All work is unto the Lord and requires a close, vital, intimate relationship with Him.

4) The combination of intimate relationship with Jesus and work is the fruitful evidence of authentic joining to Christ and His Body.

5) This depth of joining to the community of the Church is the only tangible means by which true security is lastingly felt.

In the beginning of this chapter I stated that poor, miserable Christians are tired because they are fighting God. His Spirit is trying to move them into true joy, security and freedom; they steadfastly resist God's way in order to cling to their present misery. They assume the cost is much greater than the return. I have presented the means to end this conflict and frustration. Joy and security are two elements that bring peace and rest to the struggling soul.

FREEDOM

The key to security is servanthood. The key to joy is servanthood. The same connection exists between servanthood and freedom. Servanthood to Jesus through His Church is the sole means of knowing personal, inner freedom.

Every day we serve somebody. We serve the devil or we serve the Lord. In all things we either build the kingdom of the devil or build the Kingdom of the Lord. There is no third alternative.

In the face of this fact, the word "freedom" requires redefining. Freedom is commonly thought to be independence, or full self-determination to do what we want, when we want, in the way we want and with the expected results we want. This understanding of independence is not true freedom at all, however, for only service brings true freedom. There are only two alternate and opposite opportunities for service: servanthood to sin and death or servanthood to righteousness and everlasting life.

Freedom, then, is not a license to do what we want; it is the ability to choose to serve whom we ought to serve: Christ. Freedom is the liberty to choose, or free will. This ability was not always available. Once we were in bondage to an existence of living death.

> And you He made alive, who were dead in trespasses and sins, in which you once walked according to the course of this world, according to the prince of the power of the air, the spirit who now works in the sons of disobedience, among whom also we all once conducted ourselves in the lusts of our flesh, fulfilling the desires of the flesh and of the mind, and were by nature children of wrath, just as the others.
>
> Ephesians 2:1-3

> Do you not know that to whom you present yourselves slaves to obey, you are that one's slaves whom you obey, whether of sin leading to death, or of obedience leading to righteousness? But God be thanked that though you were slaves of sin, yet you obeyed from the heart that form of doctrine to which you were delivered.
>
> Romans 6:16-17

Once we were the bondmen of lust. Now we are free. Once we were the servants of sin and death. Now we are free. We are free to serve a new Master.

Poor, miserable Christians are in bondage to serving self. In reality that means they continue to serve their old master, the devil. No wonder they are unhappy.

The truly free find their joy and security in genuine service to a new Master. They are called His disciples. Certainly from a historical standpoint, "disciple" is another word for "servant," at least in a qualified sense. This is true from the days of Socrates to Jesus to the trade guilds of the Middle Ages. Elisha, the disciple of Elijah, learned Elijah's prophetic craft because Elisha "became his servant" (I Kings 19:21) and "poured water on the hands of Elijah" (II Kings 3:11). Jesus used the words interchangeably when speaking of those who seriously followed Him. Disciples and servants are those who faithfully observe and fulfill all the commands of their master.

Jesus said to the Jews who believed Him, "If you abide in My word, you are My disciples indeed. You shall know the truth, and the truth shall make you free" (John 8:31-32). Much can be said about the truth that makes free. Certainly one part of that freedom is the ability to be disciples; indeed, to continue in servanthood as Jesus did.

Ultimately, only through servanthood is genuine freedom discovered—freedom from the misery of self-service or devil-service. Through servanthood we experience the true freedom of being servants of God in the way He uniquely created us to serve.

Further Study for Personal Enrichment

Chapter Two

1. By what key trait are poor, miserable Christians characterized, and why? Does that describe you?

2. In a half-page, differentiate between the way many Christians define joy and the proper definition and expressions of joy.

3. List the five key elements of faithful service, as derived from Jesus' parable in Matthew 25.

4. Name the three natural areas in which a Christian servant must be proven faithful.

5. Write a prayer to your Heavenly Father confessing your faults and asking for His help in the area or areas where you need to be proven faithful.

6. What happens to your heart when you sell all for the Kingdom?

7. From the illustrations of the catechism ministry and Custodial Crew, summarize, in a page, why those involved would feel security.

8. Restate the sole means of knowing personal, inner freedom.

9. Every day we serve somebody. We serve the _____ or we serve the _____ . We either build the kingdom of the _____ or build the Kingdom of the _____ . There is _____ third alternative.

10. In a paragraph, differentiate between the commonly held thought of freedom and the proper perspective on freedom.

11. To whom are poor, miserable Christians in bondage to serve?

12. Write a prayer telling your Heavenly Father what this chapter stirred in your heart for your involvement in your local church. Ask for His help in bringing your desires for servanthood into reality.

Chapter Three

Jesus, the Pattern

An important principle in theology asserts that Christianity is to be understood according to the precepts and examples of the New Testament. Precepts are the direct New Testament teachings and commands. Examples are the recorded life experiences of Christ and the apostles.

In previous chapters I discussed broad principles or precepts of servanthood. The purpose of this chapter is to understand servanthood as modelled by Christ Himself. The Lord Jesus is the pattern or model of true biblical service. He illustrates the joy, security and freedom of servanthood. As a fully human being in a fully human body, He is our example of complete, obedient, humble service. This fact demonstrates for all believers that they are capable of the same. Jesus is to be emulated, at the least, in the following nine ways.

1. Kindly service. At the heart of servanthood is the spirit of kindness. Kindness is the movement away from self that seeks to speedily bring healing, assistance and benefit to others. Service of this nature invites interruption and, indeed, always is being interrupted. Intrusion by the needy was a constant occurrence in Jesus' life.

God anointed Jesus of Nazareth with the Holy Spirit and with power, who went about doing good and healing all who were oppressed by the devil, for God was with Him.
Acts 10:38

This scripture mentions being anointed with the Holy Spirit. Today much mention is made of "the anointing." The anointing is emphasized especially in connection with corporate worship, including preaching and the ministering of spiritual gifts. Indeed, it is desperately needed there. Without the anointing, worship is valueless to God. The anointing is a prerequisite for our ability as Christ's members to have a psalm, a doctrine, a tongue, a revelation or an interpretation (I Cor. 14:26) and to worship with art and excellence in a way that truly beautifies and pleases God.

But what about the anointing as it pertains to our lives outside the public meeting? Jesus was an individual man who faced even the most routine daily tasks with the anointing of the Spirit. It can be reasonably said that at no time was Jesus unanointed. Because He is our model, the same can be true of us, if we will receive it.

The purpose of the anointing is to provide goodness and kindness. It vanquishes sorrow and pain and heals the oppressed. Because He was anointed, Jesus approached life with the mission to do good. Because Jesus performed acts of goodness and kindness, the Father revealed Himself as being with Jesus and working with Him. Jesus fulfilled what He later commanded.

Jesus, before He ascended, commissioned His disciples to "Go into all the world and preach the gospel to every creature" (Mark 16:15). These signs, He said, would follow believers who go: "In My name they will cast out demons; they will speak with new tongues; they will take up serpents; and if they drink anything deadly, it will by no means hurt them; they will lay hands on the sick, and they will recover" (vs. 17, 18). His disciples, once anointed with the Spirit, verified by experience the promise of the Master: "And they went out and preached everywhere, the Lord working with them and confirming the word through the accompanying signs" (v. 20). God worked with them. As the Father had been with Christ, He was now with Christ's Church, divinely confirming their directed mission of service.

Anointing, then, is for service. Anointed service of kindness reveals the presence of God Himself. This pattern is proven by the life testimony both of Christ and of His disciples. It is a pattern that we, too, are to prove and live.

2. Rejoicing service.

Looking unto Jesus, the author and finisher of our faith, who for the joy that was set before Him endured the cross, despising the shame, and has sat down at the right hand of the throne of God.

Hebrews 12:2

Jesus' motive for serving was for joy—both immediate and future joy. He served because of the joy that was set before Him. "Joy set *before* Him" has the same sense as David's words, "You prepare a table *before* me" (Ps. 23:5). In other words, Jesus' joy was immediate and ever-present. The present joy of serving motivated Him to greater servanthood.

Jesus served for immediate joy—for the sake of service itself—not for immediate personal acquisition or benefit. If his motivation of serving is for immediate personal comfort or preference rather than for the joy of obedience, a believer-servant does not do well in his work generally, and especially in work that requires endurance.

And which of you, having a servant plowing or tending sheep, will say to him when he has come in from the field, "Come at once and sit down to eat"? But will he not rather say to him, "Prepare something for my supper, and gird yourself and serve me till I have eaten and drunk, and afterward you will eat and drink"?

Luke 17:7-8

Too often would-be servants lose heart when fleshly or material returns or remuneration are not immediate. "I want what is coming to me and I want it now." Comparatively speaking, these words are seldom spoken aloud, but they are said regularly—and at least daily—in popular public attitude.

The would-be servant may also say or think, "Well, if there is no immediate reward for my work, at least show some appreciation. I want a little notice, a little respect." What I am about to say is a "hard saying," because we all have experienced these feelings. It is not unbiblical to long to hear the words, "Well done." But notice and respect are future and elusive and often come capriciously. Water cannot be held in a clenched fist. But a little water settles nicely into a cupped, open and yielding palm. It can be held, or experienced, indefinitely. By analogy, when we grasp for the approval and affirmation of others, we often do it with the clenched first of demand.

Unfortunately, we can never receive enough of these kind of "strokes"—notice and respect—to satisfy our need for approval. *A demanding person is never satisfied.* Instead, if we have a servant's attitude that is of open and yielded willingness, then we likely will have and feel all the admiration and recognition that we need.

Jesus' joy in serving was linked also to His anticipation and acquisition of future benefit. Jesus served for a future joy. That joy is identified in the Book of Hebrews, that He could be the Author of eternal salvation for all who will obey and so bring many sons to glory. In other words, Jesus' joy was the acquisition of saved men—those whom He calls servants, friends, brothers, daughters—the whole company of the redeemed. The degree of Jesus' own hope and joy was commensurate with His ministry of redemption through the cross.

Jesus' joy was both present and future. His immediate joy was the subjective assurance that He had obeyed God and had done God's will. Jesus' future joy was the fellowship of redeemed man. These joys provided endurance for continuing in service.

I defined joy as being connected with personal acquisition. Jesus re-defines joy. For Jesus, knowledge of personal obedience and eternal life for others are personal gain. His gain is to "advantage" others. His example teaches a serious lesson which we ought to carefully heed. Can we truly be satisfied with our role to solely promote another? Is it possible to serve with no motivation or expectation other than to prosper that person? Can we still receive fullness of joy if we so serve? Jesus' example says yes.

The key to understanding is in the opening words of Hebrews 12:2: "Looking unto Jesus." We are to fix our spiritual, mental and emotional adoring gaze on Him, the Alpha and Omega, the Beginning and the End, the Author and Finisher. He is the source. He is the means. He is the end. From this perspective, Jesus gazed on His Father for joy, endurance and the ability to perform and complete His service-mission. He said, "The Son can do nothing of Himself, but what He sees the Father do" (John 5:19). Jesus, in the servanthood of His humanity, expressed the Father because He gazed on the Father. When we believers gaze on Jesus we become like Him. We become like Him in the joy and service He modelled.

3. Tangible service.

Whoever desires to be first among you, let him be your slave; just as the Son of Man did not come to be served, but to serve, and to give His life a ransom for many.

Matthew 20:27-28

Jesus expressed tangible service. Jesus taught tangible service. Jesus lived tangible service. Notice that this scripture makes no direct reference to "heart." The heart to serve is presumed. It is the literal, visible work of service that is stressed. Many allow Jesus to live in their hearts but do not let Him live in their minds, hands, feet or tongues. Yet, the apostle James says, "Show me your faith without your works, and I will show you my faith by my works" (James 2:18).

The relationship between the work of service and the heart of service is indeed the same relationship that exists between "works" and "faith." In both verses 17 and 26, James states that faith cannot exist by itself.

Thus also faith by itself, if it does not have works, is dead.

James 2:17

For as the body without the spirit is dead, so faith without works is dead also.

James 2:26

The analogy James employs in the latter verse is that of body and spirit. The body is the outward form—the literal, visible, tangible expression of that which is without form, the spirit. The body cannot survive without spirit, or breath. When breath departs, the body dies. In the same way, outward works are the literal, visible, tangible expression of a person's inner faith. Faith is the breath, or life, behind works of enduring and godly value. Works are the evidence, or body, of that faith. When no works are present to substantiate faith, then no genuine faith is present. In that case, faith has departed as breath from a body. In order for faith to survive, it must have a body through which it can be expressed. For a servant's heart to be present, there must be real expression of the works of service.

Christianity needs a body for expression. "But a body You have prepared for Me" (Heb. 10:5). The Church is called the "Body of Christ." Certainly that metaphor establishes God's intent for us to be the outward, visible, tangible, earthly demonstration of the Lord Jesus Christ, as much as and even more than Jesus Himself expressed when He was mortally present on earth (John 14:12). Service is the practical and tangible means by which to glorify God through a body. "Glorify God in your body and in your spirit, which are God's" (I Cor. 6:20). We glorify God in spirit through worship; we glorify God in body through service.

4. Diligent service.

Therefore pray the Lord of the harvest to send out laborers into His harvest.

Matthew 9:38

Do business till I come.

Luke 19:13

Occupy. Do business. Work. Send laborers or workers. Though Matthew 9:38 is commonly used to hearten and encourage the work of soul-winning, the verse does not say, "Send evangelists."

Service is work. Service is difficult, arduous labor. It calls for enduring hardship. Jesus was unafraid of work. The work of the cross and His atoning death are His primary service to man. As a man, Christ took on the form of a servant. Why? To humble Himself and become obedient to death, even to death on the cross.

"Let this same mind be in you which was also in Christ Jesus" (Phil. 2:5). Believers do not follow in the steps of Christ to help Him atone for the world's sins. Atonement was Jesus' own unique ministry, not able to be duplicated by any other. But believers are to imitate the steps of Christ, and His character and actions in particular.

If anyone desires to come after Me, let him deny himself, and take up his cross, and follow Me. For whoever desires to save his life will lose it, but whoever loses his life for My sake will find it.

Matthew 16:24-25

The hard work of service that Christ bore daily in denying Himself, taking His cross and following His Father's leading to Calvary is the same kind of hard work that lies before every one of Christ's servants. Jesus the man, as forerunner, proves that even the severity of His service is not beyond the power of the servants who follow after Him in order to be like Him.

5. Humble service.

He who is greatest among you shall be your servant. And whoever exalts himself will be humbled, and he who humbles himself will be exalted.

Matthew 23:11-12

The very word "servant" brings to mind pictures of lowliness and humility. Jesus said in His parable, "Well done, good and faithful servant" (Matt. 25:21, 23). He did not say, "Well done, good administrator," or "Well done, faithful pastor," or elder or deacon. The way up is down. Grasping for position only hinders growth in Christ. Humble yourselves, the Bible says (James 4:10; I Pet. 5:6). When we do, God places us in the appropriate position of service. God promotes according to His timing and according to that servant's qualifications before Him.

"Before honor is humility," affirms Proverbs 15:33. Follow Christ and allow God to bring the honor whenever He deems it is due. Practice humility. Jesus did. He walked fully on that path. He never felt the need to stand up for Himself or to convince others of His greatness.

Great multitudes followed Him, and He healed them all. Yet He warned them not to make Him known, that it might be fulfilled which was spoken by Isaiah the prophet, saying: "Behold! My Servant whom I have

*chosen, My Beloved in whom My soul is well pleased! I
will put My Spirit upon Him, and He will declare justice to the Gentiles. He will not quarrel nor cry out, nor
will anyone hear His voice in the streets. A bruised reed
He will not break, and smoking flax He will not quench,
till He sends forth justice to victory.*

Matthew 12:15-20

Early in His life, Jesus decided that He would not
grasp at any ambition. Being God Himself, Jesus willingly relinquished all deity (position) to become a man.
Being a man, He did not allow Himself to consider grasping equality with God. That is why, after Jesus' atoning
death...

*God also has highly exalted Him and given Him the
name which is above every name, that at the name of
Jesus every knee should bow, of those in heaven, and of
those on earth, and of those under the earth, and that
every tongue should confess that Jesus Christ is Lord, to
the glory of God the Father.*

Philippians 2:9-11

Whatever Jesus did as a man, He showed His followers that they, as men, could also do. "I have given you
an example, that you should do as I have done to you"
(John 13:15). Whether or not Christians obey, the principle
remains constant: Because Jesus did it, His followers are
called to do it. "As He is, so are we in this world" (I John
4:17).

As formidable a task as it may sound, we must con-
front our attitudes regarding the distress, or perceived
distress, of serving—the labor and thanklessness involved in light of the modest, selfless spirit we are enjoined to have. We dare not neglect confronting wrong

44

attitudes; otherwise, we are playing Christianity while denying its power. Playing Christianity causes us to become sons and daughters, not of Christ, but of the scribes and Pharisees who spurned Him for the security of religious tradition. Through any and all distress our prevailing attitude must be: I am privileged to serve. I am awed by the honor He has bestowed in considering me worthy to serve. By my serving I show to all the very greatness of my Lord Jesus Christ.

This attitude is possible. Each one of us who are Christ's has His power for living. If it were not so, the following commands would never have been written:

For I say, through the grace given to me, to everyone who is among you, not to think of himself more highly than he ought to think, but to think soberly, as God has dealt to each one a measure of faith.

Romans 12:3

Be of the same mind toward one another. Do not set your mind on high things, but associate with the humble. Do not be wise in your own opinion.

Romans 12:16

Humility does not resist obedience to these scriptures. True humility revives, refreshes and rejuvenates. Consider yourself, in your experience with the Lord when you first resisted Him, and afterward became convicted, broken and repentant and said, "Yes." You understand and have found in humility a peaceful and deeply satisfying state. You know it as a spiritual dwelling place of safety, refuge and fulfillment to which you may ever return. God Himself dwells there. He resists the proud, but He discloses Himself in the presence of the humble spirit and in the heart of the contrite ones (Isa. 57:15). The

Kingdom of heaven is promised by Jesus to such poor in spirit.

6. Willing service.

I delight to do Your will, O my God.

Psalm 40:8

For I have come down from heaven, not to do My own will, but the will of Him who sent Me.

John 6:38

Jesus is the pattern of willing, ready service. A good example of this attitude and behavior is that of the gentleman's gentleman: the valet. Although now considered a dying profession in North America, domestic service is certainly one of the oldest of man's occupations. Indeed, in some regions it is still a thriving and needed profession. The principles observed from this profession are life lessons all believers should heed. Christ was truly the supreme gentleman's gentleman to His Father.

A gentleman's gentleman devotes himself entirely to the service, convenience and pleasure of another. Jesus did not live for Himself (Rom. 15:3), but for the Father (John 6:57). Let's look at how Jesus fulfilled this service.

Gentleman's Gentleman	Jesus
Is chiefly concerned with his master's appearance.	"I have glorified You on the earth" (John 17:4).
Guards the door of his master's home.	"I am the door" (John 10:9). "I am the way, the truth, and the life. No one comes to the Father except through Me" (John 14:6).

Gentleman's Gentleman	Jesus
Does errands for his master.	"I have come down from heaven, not to do My own will, but the will of Him who sent Me" (John 6:38).
Has power of attorney.	"The works that I do in My Father's name, they bear witness of Me" (John 10:25).
Refreshes his master with food and beverage.	"I always do those things that please Him" (John 8:29).
Heads the household staff.	Christ is both servant and Son over all His Father's house (Heb. 3:5-6).
Manages his master's household affairs.	"I must be about My Father's business" (Luke 2:49).
Is always "on duty."	"As long as I am in the world, I am the light of the world" (John 9:5).

7. Unpresuming service.

Father, if it is Your will, take this cup away from Me; nevertheless not My will, but Yours, be done.

Luke 22:42

Jesus did not presume with God. He esteemed God's will as more important than His own. Knowing and doing God's will were supremely and solely important. Nothing else mattered. When Jesus was uncertain, He sought His Father until He became certain.

There is no better New Testament example of this than Jesus' prayer in the Garden of Gethsemane. This moment in history was critical; Jesus was facing imminent crucifixion. Was now to be the time? Was this to be the way? The burden of responsibility felt by the Lord was greater than any other would ever bear. The redemption of all humanity was at stake. Nothing less than absolute confidence of direction was needed by Jesus. He had said, "Ask, and it will be given to you; seek, and you will find; knock, and it will be opened to you" (Matt. 7:7). Here in the Garden with none but His closest intimates nearby, Jesus Himself asked and kept on asking in prayer.

He prayed once; He prayed twice; but His agony continued so that His sweat was like great drops of blood (Luke 22:44). Even ministry by an angel (v. 43) was insufficient to meet His need. Only a direct answer from God, His Father, would do. He pursued God until He received His answer; Jesus knew what would now happen:

He came the third time and said to them, "Are you still sleeping and resting? It is enough! The hour has come; behold the Son of Man is being betrayed into the hands of sinners. Rise, let us be going. See, My betrayer is at hand."

Mark 14:41-42

Many Christian servants may be called to face crises similar in either degree or kind. They cannot do without this same kind of praying. Knowledge and study of the Scriptures is essential throughout all life and work, of course. But how are believers to apply the principles of the Word? What principles are they to make use of, and in which situations? In what order are the principles to be applied, and to what degree? What about God's timing? Are there any other considerations? Answers to hard questions are obtained in the prayer closet.

Service that is unassuming requires the mind of the Master. It requires confidence in the Master's mind. It is knowing what He would do and the way that He would do it.

I once made a poster for my church members that read, "What would Jesus have me do?" Later I realized that God calls us to have knowledge of a higher quality. The poster remains the same, except the words "have" and "me" are crossed out.

No Christian service can exist without a relationship that brings such knowledge of the Master. As Jesus Himself was with His Father, so are we to be with Jesus.

8. Instant and unrestrained service.

He sat down, called the twelve, and said to them, "If anyone desires to be first, he shall be last of all and servant of all."

Mark 9:35

Yet it shall not be so among you; but whoever desires to become great among you shall be your servant. And whoever of you desires to be first shall be slave of all. For even the Son of Man did not come to be served, but to serve, and to give His life a ransom for many.

Mark 10:43-45

An important attitude of any true servant is that of instant response to orders given. Instant and unrestrained service was the way of Jesus. He exemplified instant obedience to His Father. God is our loving Father as well. What parent would not wish first-time obedience to be the heart and behavior response of his or her children? First-time obedience means to obey the command the first time it is given. If the command needs to be given a second time, then second-time obedience is taught. First-time obedience is possible because it is the pattern shown by Jesus.

The two scriptures quoted at the opening of this section are from the Gospel of Mark. The Christian symbol for Mark's Gospel is the ox, the loyal, steady, serving beast of burden. The key word of the Gospel of Mark is "immediately." The word and its synonyms are used more than forty times to describe the actions of Jesus. He knew this secret: The greatest gain is acquired through the greatest service; therefore, the greatest gain is when service is unrestrained.

9. **Loving service.** First Corinthians 13 is appropriately called the love chapter of the Bible. It also may rightly be called the service chapter, since functional love is dying to self in serving another. Indeed, love is service and service is love. There cannot be one without the other. By replacing the word "love" with "service" or "servant," First Corinthians 13 reads:

> *Though I speak with the tongues of men and of angels, but am not a servant, I have become sounding brass or a clanging cymbal. And though I have the gift of prophecy, and understand all mysteries and all knowledge, and though I have all faith, so that I could remove mountains, but am not a servant, I am nothing. And though I*

bestow all my goods to feed the poor, and though I give
my body to be burned, but am not servant, it profits me
nothing. Service suffers long and is kind; service does
not envy; service does not parade itself, is not puffed
up; does not behave rudely, does not seek its own, is
not provoked, thinks no evil; does not rejoice in iniquity,
but rejoices in the truth; bears all things, believes all
things, hopes all things, endures all things. Service
never fails. But whether there are prophecies, they will
fail; whether there are tongues, they will cease; whether
there is knowledge, it will vanish away. And now abide
faith, hope, service, these three; but the greatest of these
is service.

Jesus, of course, is the pattern of loving service. He fulfilled its meaning in the ideal sense. As said of every other aspect where Jesus is our pattern, He modelled for us that which we are to imitate. To love by serving in the degree that Jesus loved is both possible and essential.

Jesus said, "No longer do I call you servants, for a servant does not know what his master is doing; but I have called you friends, for all things that I heard from My Father I have made known to you" (John 15:15). These words seem peculiar and contradictory in light of this discussion. They are not. Service to Jesus as demonstrated through service to others is the prerequisite to and fulfillment of the love relationship called friendship. He said, "You are My friends if you do whatever I command you" (John 15:14). Doing whatever is commanded is serving. Servanthood earns the right of, not salvation, but Jesus' friendship.

In Philippians 2:5-8 the apostle Paul calls believers to adopt Jesus' mentality. Servanthood is a command, or precept. But the servanthood Christians are to adopt, Paul says, is that which Christ Himself exemplified. There could be no such New Testament command of following Jesus' example if Jesus' followers were incapable of obeying. Inherent in the commands of God are sufficient graces to obey in a way that is pleasing to Him.

If we have studied the model of Jesus, the servant, through the eyes of inadequacy—"Oh, I could never be as perfect as Jesus"—then we have misinterpreted His whole reason for being our pattern. We need to re-read this chapter through new eyes, ones through which we can receive inspiration and power for living. The goal, though challenging, is the ever-positive and energizing obedient attainment and expression of Christ's own life. The goal is never a disobedient expression of inadequacy and excuse-making. Instead, it is possible to be like Jesus by following His pattern of service. All His power and provision are at our disposal.

Further Study for Personal Enrichment

Chapter Three

1. List the nine ways that Jesus is to be emulated.

2. Identify the purpose of the anointing.

3. How was Jesus' joy both present and future?

4. Explain, in a brief paragraph, how "looking unto Jesus" can help you in your service.

5. Jesus _____ , _____

   and _____ tangible service.

6. What do outward works express?

7. Cite the kind of work that lies before you as one
   of Christ's servants.

8. Restate the result of grasping for position in the
   Body of Christ.

9. In your own words, write a paragraph showing how Jesus was a gentleman's gentleman.

10. What does unassuming service require?

11. In a paragraph, give an example of a time when you served both instantly and unrestrainedly. Thank God for this opportunity to do His will.

12. Servanthood earns the right of, not salvation, but Jesus' _____ .

13. Don't be discouraged by Jesus' perfected model of servanthood as described in this chapter. Instead, write a heart-felt prayer expressing to Him which of the nine areas where you feel inadequate and asking Him for specific ways in which you can better emulate His servanthood.

Chapter Four

No Choice
But to Serve the King

Where is the Kingdom of God? It is in heaven, certainly, but it is also on earth. Bringing Christ's Kingdom on earth is the prayer of every saint who follows Jesus' command to pray His model prayer. "Your kingdom come," we Christians daily say. "Your will be done on earth as it is in heaven" (Matt. 6:10). Jesus does not taunt us by commanding us to so pray. The reality of His ever-expanding Kingdom on earth ought to be the earnest labor and certain expectancy of every believer. I find that this portion of the Lord's Prayer is a personal affirmation of servanthood and a subjection to cooperate with His rule and dominion, to express it and to not be found an enemy.

A king is often thought of in relation to three groups: his servants, citizens and enemies. (Many Christians wish for three such groups.) Servants would be those especially close to the king, under his direct employ. They would include his army, the keepers of his estate and the conductors of his affairs. Enemies, of course, would be those outside the kingdom, manifesting opposing ideas and having opposing loyalties. But, the king's citizens would constitute the great majority of the kingdom. They would be the decent folk who pay their taxes. They would be patriotic and openly support his rule. They would be grateful recipients of all kingdom benefits and programs. But apart from the king, they would be about their own concerns. "Live and let live," they would say. "Things that I choose to do that are within my own rights are no one's business but mine."

The reign of our God and Christ is eternal and absolute in heaven and in earth. Though it may not be seen, it is true. He is Lord of all. He reigns eternally and sovereignly now. Though I may not like it, the New Testament presents His lordship over two kinds of people only: His servants and His enemies.

So there is no third group. Men are either servants with servants' hearts or enemies of the King at heart. "He who is not with Me is against Me, and he who does not gather with Me scatters abroad" (Matt. 12:30). Anyone who puts himself in a third category ought to fear lest the King deem him to be an opponent. To quote Luther, "Unless a man serves only God, then he will surely serve the devil."[1]

The Kingdom of God, then, encompasses two groups. First, the Kingdom is Christ's Church, the visible colony of heaven on earth. The Kingdom is the collective body of servants. They live to please their Lord by thought, deed and word. Their servanthood is evidenced by their actions; their deeds openly testify to what it means to be living in harmony with Christ's direct rule.

---

1. Scheidt, David L. ed., *Martin Luther's Table-Talk*, *"The True Service of God,"* The World Publishing Company, Cleveland, 1969 (First Printing).

Who then is a faithful and wise servant, whom his master made ruler over his household, to give them food in due season? Blessed is that servant whom his master, when he comes, will find so doing. Assuredly, I say to you that he will make him ruler over all his goods.

Matthew 24:45-47

Second, the Kingdom of God is over all. God's rule knows no bounds, either in space or in time. Those who utterly or habitually refuse to cooperate with His direct rule are His enemies, even though they still live within the borders of the Kingdom. The wheat and the tares grow together in the same field (Matt. 13:30). For now, enemies enjoy His longsuffering, patience and mercy. The King awaits their repentance. King Jesus desires for all to be saved, turned from being enemies in heart to be servants and friends. A person's heart attitude will ultimately be confronted either by his repentance or by the King's judgment.

But if that evil servant says in his heart, "My master is delaying his coming," and begins to beat his fellow servants, and to eat and drink with the drunkards, the master of that servant will come on a day when he is not looking for him and at an hour that he is not aware of, and will cut him in two and appoint him his portion with the hypocrites. There shall be weeping and gnashing of teeth.

Matthew 24:48-51

The message of servanthood instructs us on how to live in Jesus' Kingdom as a servant, not as an enemy. Four fundamental principles for Kingdom servanthood must be recognized.

1. Servanthood is a command. A king makes his decree. Obedience is required. All servants obey. Those who habitually do not obey—whose chosen practice is sin—are not, or are no longer, his servants. The Lord knows His servants by their evident obedience (action). Servants know for themselves that they are servants because of their obedience. Obedience is required from both perspectives. Obedience involves actively doing, not just mental assent. "Therefore by their fruits you will know them" (Matt. 7:20). Obedience establishes whom a servant serves.

> *Do you not know that to whom you present yourselves slaves to obey, you are that one's slaves whom you obey, whether of sin leading to death, or of obedience leading to righteousness?*
>
> Romans 6:16

2. Servanthood is a choice. Because it is an eternal decree, servanthood to Christ is absolute. *One cannot absolutely reject servanthood and remain a Christian.* Because man's free will is eternally decreed, servanthood is conditional and progressive. How can this be? Though a king decrees, his servants must choose. *Men are in character and in destiny the product of their life choices.*

Christ described two, and only two, kingdoms: one of servants and one of enemies. The division is absolute. Servanthood choices determine in which absolute a Christian remains. He made his faith-choice at the beginning to obey the gospel and enter Christ's Kingdom of servants. He must daily make his faith-choice to continue as a servant of Christ. If this were not true, Joshua never would have confronted redeemed and victorious Israel.

His words of command are an abiding challenge for every believer: "Choose for yourselves this day whom you will serve" (Josh. 24:15).

Servanthood is a daily choice. Therefore, its results are progressive and expansive in the life of the servant. So servanthood is essential for personal growth, and growth means increased service. "Essential" means "required, absolutely necessary." If you take away service, you take away growth.

Food is eaten to fuel the capacity to work. Work expends energy and requires more fuel. The entire process is one of at least maintaining and hopefully increasing work capacity. That is why Paul says, "We commanded you this: If anyone will not work, neither shall he eat" (II Thess. 3:10). It is an eternal law expressed in many ways: "You shall not muzzle an ox while it treads out the grain" and "The laborer is worthy of his wages" (I Tim. 5:18). There should be no privileges without responsibilities.

I should note here the distinctions between two important New Testament words for service. The first word is *diakonos*; the second word is *doulos*. *Diakonos* is most likely derived from an obscure root meaning "to run on errands." A *diakonos* is an attendant, a waiter on tables, a performer of menial duties. The word may be used to describe a teacher or pastor. Most often it refers to the person designated to be a deacon or deaconess in a church. *Diakonos* is translated "deacon," "minister" and "servant."

Doulos is a slave without rights. Literally, he is a man in bonds or chains, forced to his labor. He is wholly the property of another. The word may be used in a literal or figurative sense, and of voluntary or involuntary servitude. *Doulos* is translated "bond," "bondman" and "servant."

The two words illustrate differences of servants, both in kind and in degree. An example of *diakonos* is found in John 12:26:

> *If anyone serves Me, let him follow Me; and where I am, there My servant will be also. If anyone serves Me, him My Father will honor.*

Doulos is used by Paul in Romans 6:16:

> *Do you not know that to whom you present yourselves slaves to obey, you are that one's slaves whom you obey, whether of sin leading to death, or of obedience leading to righteousness?*

Although each word may be applied either positively or negatively (the role of deacon is a *positive* ministry; bondslaves to sin lead a *negative* lifestyle), it is common to draw unfavorable inference from *diakonos* and favorable from *doulos*. Let me explain these distinctions, as I see them.

Service of a *diakonos* is voluntary, imposed by self and terminated by self. Its limits are defined by self. On the other hand, the service of a *doulos* is involuntary. His service has no beginning and no ending. Terms are established and enforced by others.

The mind of the *diakonos* is set on the blessing due at the end of his service. He is a hireling. He works for reward in whatever form it may come. In the end, the servant is exalted. In contrast, the mind of the *doulos* is set on the word and authority of his master. He is owned. He lives for the benefit and promotion of another. The final result of his work exalts his master.

The character of the *diakonos* is demonstrated by the quality of work accomplished. The character of the *doulos* is shown by his relationship with his master and by the quality of the work he accomplishes.

The *diakonos* is illustrative of "the American way": independence, personal rights, freedom and democracy based on individual rights and free will. The *diakonos* thinks, "The church had better appreciate what I have to give." The *doulos* exemplifies a lifestyle of the way of the redeemed. He does nothing but follow the Lamb wherever He may go (Rev. 14:4). Although he has a free will, he has so fully yielded it to the will of his master that it is swallowed up by the master's.

The *diakonos* serves when he feels like it. The *doulos* serves because of his nature. He cannot restrain service.

The *diakonos* makes many choices based on personal gain and personal gratification whenever he is off duty— and most American Christians are "off duty" a lot of the time. The *doulos* is never off duty. He has no regard for his own interests. He lives to be at his master's disposal. Apart from his master, he considers himself to be nothing. He is totally secure because he is totally owned.

The believer who lives entirely as a *diakonos* is risking enmity with God. Doing "in part" the service and works of the Father is not identical with doing the will of the Father. "Doing" service does not mean you "are" a servant. I repeat, however, that although the flesh produces nothing worthwhile, it does not disqualify. It is better to obey in service "in the flesh" than to disobey and ensure one's status as an enemy of God.

> *Not everyone who says to Me, "Lord, Lord," shall enter the kingdom of heaven, but he who does the will of My Father in heaven. Many will say to Me in that day, "Lord, Lord, have we not prophesied in Your name, cast out demons in Your name, and done many wonders in Your name?" And then I will declare to them, "I never knew you; depart from Me, you who practice lawlessness!"*
>
> Matthew 7:21-23

At best, being a *diakonos* is being on the pathway to becoming a *doulos*. *Doulos* includes every positive quality of *diakonos*, but ever so much more. Most congregations are thrilled to have a few with *diakonos* attributes; they have little vision of the higher dimension of *doulos*. One can be a *diakonos* and never be a *doulos*. But one could never be a *doulos* without possessing all the positive attributes of a *diakonos*. To say it another way, it is possible to be obedient, but not from the heart. It is not possible to be a servant in heart without obeying. The one comes as naturally from the other as works follow faith. Of course, God's desire for His Church is to raise up a corporate *doulos* with a geniune heart to serve.

Young John Knox knew he was a man with Christ's call on him when he was captured by the French and made a galley slave. Eventually he escaped. But there below deck, bound in chains, subject to beatings and forced to labor, Knox learned lessons from the School of Christ. Though he seldom spoke of that time, there is no doubt that his experience was of lasting impact. While preparing to be a *diakonos*, God made him into a *doulos*.

3. Servanthood is the only choice. Not only is servanthood a choice, we must also see it as the only choice, the sole alternative, for that is what it is. It continues the idea of servanthood being a command. We servants get into trouble when we take a command and make it an option.

> *Now it happened as they journeyed on the road, that someone said to Him, "Lord, I will follow You wherever You go." And Jesus said to him, "Foxes have holes and birds of the air have nests, but the Son of Man has nowhere to lay His head." Then He said to another, "Follow Me." But he said, "Lord, let me first go and bury my father." Jesus said to him, "Let the dead bury their own dead, but you go and preach the kingdom of God." And another also said, "Lord, I will follow You, but let me first go and bid them farewell who are at my house." But Jesus said to him, "No one, having put his hand to the plow, and looking back, is fit for the kingdom of God."*
>
> Luke 9:57-62

Three different times Jesus communicates a single message: Make your choice once and for all; and after making that choice, never look back. Jesus is uncompromising on the issue of double-mindedness. Christianity is to be a single choice where its outcome determines the result of every decision ever to be faced. There is to be no wavering between non-existant alternatives. One choice is to fit all.

In this regard, "Remember Lot's wife" (Luke 17:32) is a stern warning that still applies today. Her vacillation toward an alternative that did not exist caused her to be wasted, useless to God and to man. Or, to paraphrase from Hebrews 11:15-16, if we begin to seriously call to mind and focus our attention on that lifestyle from which we were saved, it is possible that we could be given an opportunity to return. However, in truth, we desire a better, heavenly lifestyle.

One other excellent biblical example of this one-choice concept is found in the laws regarding betrothal and marriage. Paul says of believers in his care, "I am jealous for you with godly jealousy. For I have betrothed you to one husband, that I may present you as a chaste virgin to Christ" (II Cor. 11:2). The impact of his words, however, is lost because of inadequate understanding of the words betrothed or espoused. Today's common definition of betrothal or espousal is engagement to marry. But the biblical definition is marriage itself—every part of it—except its consummation. Espousal includes all vows of commitment and completion of the contract between the individuals and their families. If an espoused bride or bridegroom was discovered to be a fornicator, then that person, according to God's law, was an adulterer and worthy of death.

If a young woman who is a virgin is betrothed to a husband, and a man finds her in the city and lies with her, then you shall bring them both out to the gate of that city, and you shall stone them to death with stones, the young woman because she did not cry out in the city, and the man because he humbled his neighbor's wife; so you shall put away the evil from among you. But if a man finds a betrothed young woman in the countryside, and the man forces her and lies with her, then only the man who lay with her shall die.

Deuteronomy 22:23-25

This understanding clarifies the profound and serious intention of Paul's sentiment in Second Corinthians 11:2. Christians are already married to Christ. All too frequently, though, we believe and live otherwise. But that does not alter the truth. Vows have been exchanged; the contract was ratified in blood. The choice is made. Everything the believer has belongs to Christ. Everything Christ has belongs to the believer. Nothing is owned privately. No longer is life private or personal for either bride or groom. The day of the marriage feast with its celebration and consummation is anticipated and prepared. As an ascension gift ministry, Paul sees his role as one of involvement to prepare, maintain and present the individual believer holy, spotless and blameless to Christ; to see that nothing should be found unworthy for His consummate presence.

To allow choices that the marriage contract to Christ does not permit is to stoop to adultery and desecrate the holy. Once the choice is made, any and all other alternatives—for example, the alternative not to serve—are eliminated. Joshua made his choice and rested on it for all time. "As for me and my house," he said, "we will serve the Lord" (Josh. 24:15).

4. Borders of Christ's Kingdom are to be expanded.

Joshua commanded the officers of the people, saying, "Pass through the camp and command the people, saying, 'Prepare provisions for yourselves, for within three days you will cross over this Jordan, to go in to possess the land which the LORD your God is giving you to possess.' ... But you shall pass before your brethren armed, all your might men of valor, and help them, until

*the LORD has given your brethren rest, as He gave you,
and they also have taken possession of the land which the
LORD your God is giving them. Then you shall return to
the land of your possession and enjoy it, which Moses
the LORD'S servant gave you on this side of the Jordan
toward the sunrise."*

Joshua 1:10-11; 14-15

What we believe determines how we live. Individuals
who, though married to Christ, believe themselves to be
less than married to Christ will indeed live in less than its
provision. The same thought holds true for all of Christ's
servant people. The quotation from Joshua relates to the
entrance of all Israel in possessing the inheritance of land
the Lord had promised. Israel was a theocracy; they were
ruled by Jehovah Himself. Of Israel it was said that "the
LORD his God is with him, and the shout of a king is
among them" (Num. 23:21).

When was Israel truly the people of God? Was it
before they crossed over Jordan? Was it after they had
gained victory in Canaan? They were fully God's people
before and after. The covenant was agreed and ratified on
Sinai forty years before. Astonishing evidence of God's
unlimited provision was witnessed everywhere: bread
from heaven, the rock that followed them, water from
that rock, shoes and clothes that never wore out, health
and healing and miraculous physical strength. Israel was
fully the people of God whenever they heard, believed
and obeyed what the Lord commanded. Now let's consider a perspective not commonly taught: The generation
that entered the land were overcomers prior to their entry,
especially the Reubenites, Gadites and the half tribe of

Manasseh. Joshua spoke to them in particular. Why were they important?

Two and one-half tribes had eyes that could see the inheritance from God. They refused to believe for themselves less than the full provision God would allow. Before they ever reached Jordan, the land of promise was before them. They were ready to seize all that God had for them. They did indeed seize upon it. They believed their God, and as a servant people to Him they carefully obeyed His voice. What they believed determined how they lived.

They risked appearing presumptive, and Moses challenged them for that. But Moses became convinced that their purpose was of God. Though they conquered and owned the promised land before the others, the two and one-half tribes were unwilling to settle into their portions until they had joined in winning identical provision for the rest of the nation.

The history of the tribes is analogous to our inheritance as servants in Christ's Kingdom. The fullness of Christ's provision is promised and expected. It is normal Christian life. Christians do not need to wait until death. In fact, the provision of Christ is not necessary after death. Christians need the provision of Christ in order to live *now*.

Blessed be the God and Father of our Lord Jesus Christ, who has blessed us with every spiritual blessing in the heavenly places in Christ.

Ephesians 1:3

You He made alive, who were dead in trespasses and sins, and raised us up together, and made us sit together in the heavenly places in Christ Jesus.

Ephesians 2:1, 6

For in Him dwells all the fullness of the Godhead bodily; and you are complete in Him, who is the head of all principality and power.

Colossians 2:9-10

If then you were raised with Christ, seek those things which are above, where Christ is, sitting at the right hand of God. Set your mind on things above, not on things on the earth. For you died, and your life is hidden with Christ in God.

Colossians 3:1-3

These verses are not for the future. They are for *now*. The Father has already blessed believing Christians with every spiritual blessing in the heavenlies in Christ. There is no single available heavenly blessing with which He has not already blessed His people. Expanding the borders of the Kingdom of Christ means to so totally make use of His provision that we productively win others to Him and effectively develop spiritually ourselves. Too many have the expectation that they must wait until death and heaven before they may experience the inheritance of heaven. This is wrong thinking. The provision of the inheritance from heaven is not dependent on our death but on Christ's. He died in order for Christians to become inheritors. Fullness of servanthood is available now.

I may be treading on your eschatology by urging these concepts, but I am much more concerned about "practicology" than eschatology. Christians must understand God's call for obedience today. Fullness of provision necessitates fullness of practiced obedience.

The call of Kingdom servants is to expand the borders of Christ's Kingdom, to reproduce their spirit of servanthood in others. Make disciples, Jesus said. Servants are to teach others how to observe and obey all Jesus' commands, or in other words, to become His servants (Matt. 28:19-20). Paul calls for the same action:

The things that you have heard from me among many witnesses, commit these to faithful men who will be able to teach others also.

II Timothy 2:2

The mission of church leadership includes evangelism. Evangelism is necessary, but it is not all of Christianity. It is a means to an end. Maturity, not evangelism, is the end. The mission of church leaders is...

The equipping of the saints for the work of ministry, for the edifying of the body of Christ, till we all come to the unity of the faith and of the knowledge of the Son of God, to a perfect man, to the measure of the stature of the fullness of Christ.

Ephesians 4:12-13

The result is a perfect, complete, strong man or Body of Christ. Every Christian is to be patterned after Jesus, the Servant of all. The primary objective of ministry is to develop a servant's heart in every Christian, to equip him and to place him in the function of service. Service is ministry. Every Christian in the Kingdom must be and grow as a servant. Servants who have gone before do as Reuben, Gad and Manasseh did: They join in producing for others what they have spiritually won for themselves.

In concluding this chapter, it is important to note a unique correlation between two otherwise unrelated verses in the Book of John. Both references picture Jesus' heart for servants to be with Him in His personal presence.

71

If anyone serves Me, let him follow Me; and where I am, there My servant will be also. If anyone serves Me, him My Father will honor.

John 12:26

In My Father's house are many mansions; if it were not so, I would have told you. I go to prepare a place for you. And if I go and prepare a place for you, I will come again and receive you to Myself; that where I am, there you may be also.

John 14:2-3

These may be paraphrased as such: "Follow me," Jesus says, "in service and in everything seek to serve Me. Do so, and My Father will honor you in this way: In His house or Kingdom there are many places to stay, many kinds and degrees of service in which to dwell. If it were different, I would have told you otherwise. While I was here, I occupied many places of opportunity for service. In My departure I vacated, and thereby prepared for you, those places of opportunity. I prepared a place of serving that is patterned after Me. Follow Me. I will come to you and receive you fully to Myself in the perfect place of serving. Where I am, there will My servant be. That is what I wish, that in the place I am you may fully be, and may fully be with Me."

The end of all Kingdom service is the stature or "dwelling place" of the servanthood of Jesus Himself.

Further Study for Personal Enrichment

Chapter Four

1. Men are either _____ with servants' hearts or _____ of the king at heart. Luther stated, "Unless a man serves only _____ , then he will surely serve the _____ ."

2. Write a paragraph describing the Kingdom of God.

3. List the four fundamental principles for Kingdom servanthood.

4. How do you know for yourself that you are, or are not, a servant of God?

5. Why should you choose to be a servant?

6. In a paragraph or more, contrast the words *diakonos* and *doulos*.

7. Restate God's desire for His Church.

8. Cite the result of making a command an option.

9. As a Christian, what do you need to live *now*? Upon whose death is that dependant? In your own words, rewrite the following: "Fullness of provision necessitates fullness of practiced obedience."

10. What is the primary objective of ministry?

11. Every Christian in the Kingdom _____ be and grow as a servant.

12. In a half-page, express how this chapter convinced you of your personal mandate: No choice but to serve the King.

Chapter Five

The Need for a Forgotten Solution

When asked, "What are the signs of a restored, sanctified, Spirit-filled, New Testament church?" one teacher plainly answered, "Trouble." Problems. Sin. Sins of ignorance. Refusal to live biblically.

Trying to list all the problems facing the Church today goes beyond the scope of this chapter. However, I do propose to share several areas that particularly concern me as a shepherd of a local church. A perspective on these challenges will prepare our heart to appreciate and receive the servanthood solution God provides.

1. Pastors are overworked. Often pastors are overworked because they assume the responsibilities of their people. Leaders of local churches are notorious for misunderstanding their God-given job description:

*And He Himself gave some to be apostles, some prophets, some evangelists, and some pastors and teachers, **for the equipping of the saints for the work of ministry**, for the edifying of the body of Christ, till we* *all come to the unity of the faith and of the knowledge of the Son of God, to a perfect man, to the measure of the stature of the fullness of Christ.*

Ephesians 4:11-13 (Emphasis added.)

The role of the leader as described by Paul is to effectively train and equip people for service and work. God's man or woman is supposed to create an environment for evangelism and for maturing. A local church shepherd is supposed to inspire, encourage, administrate and exhort, but is not supposed to do the people's work. The people are to do the work. Unequivocally, a pastor's leadership excellence ought to be measured in the excellence of his followers—their equipping, their skill, their heart of service and their actual service ("the work of ministry").

Why do pastors do their people's work and not their own work, as assigned by the Lord? Church tradition is certainly a factor. The common mind-set of a minister and his church members is that he is a hired go-between for men and God. Familiar liturgical routine perpetuates this myth because the pastor approaches the altar of worship while the people passively observe from their pews. The idea, "You go to God for us, Pastor, so we don't have to," began with Moses and the people of the Exodus. It still continues today.

This idea is generalized to include all Christian service. Not only is the pastor to preach and preside at the altar, his presumed duty is also to evangelize, instruct catechism, prepare candidates for confirmation, hold meetings for youth, conduct a new members' class, call on church families, visit the sick and elderly, counsel the troubled, comfort the grieving, dispense discretionary funds, have a powerful personal devotional life and, perhaps, clean the facility and print the bulletin. That is not to mention heal the sick, raise the dead, cast out demons, marry, bury and baptize. "You do the work of Christian service, Pastor, and we'll pay you" is a common attitude.

The work of ministry is the job of the people, not of the pastor. His service, along with the other four offices of the ascension gift ministries, is to cause his people to become servants. (For the sake of this discussion the term "pastor" may represent the action of any of the fivefold ministries of the Church.) Pastors or leaders who take all the work to themselves exceed the bounds of their purpose as stated by Paul (Eph. 4), and steal the people's rightful role.

2. Pastors work improperly. Pastors work improperly when they allow their comprehension of Christian service to be too narrow. They mistake one or two parts of the gospel for the whole counsel of God, or they emphasize one or two parts to the minimizing or excluding of others. Typical examples are the ministry of evangelism and the ministry of preaching. There is nothing wrong and everything right about evangelism and preaching, but by themselves they cannot fully equip, establish, mature or lead a saint to servanthood. Other aspects of the gospel are needed.

Jesus said, "These you ought to have done, without leaving the others undone" (Matt. 23:23). Jesus' point in this scripture is that both tithes and "the weightier matters of the law" are necessary; one is not to substitute for the other. My point is similar. All aspects of the gospel, not one or two, are necessary to produce healthy, mature, functioning, serving saints and an alive, healthy local church.

Local churches with limited, specialized ministries can expertly meet legitimate, select, specialized needs; but they fail to present God's whole counsel which can edify the whole man and bring forth to reality the whole image of Christ. Just as individuals within a church need those with differing strengths to cover their weaknesses, so each individual congregation, cognizant of ministry weaknesses, ought to join itself to other congregations who have the needed ministry strengths.

3. People are uncommitted. People are uncommitted because they are uninvolved. In a day when all seek to gain significance through promoting self, the relational dynamics and recognized effects of involvement in the local church afford members a legitimate, God-ordained significance and sense of worth. Since God has given to each person the need to feel valuable, He also has provided a proper and legitimate means of fulfilling this need. Involvement confirms, strengthens and establishes the commitment a believer has made to the Lord in heaven. It is a requirement of membership of His Body on earth, and it is total. The New Testament clearly testifies that neither community action nor interaction was ever considered a part-time option. Those who are not committed in action are not committed.

And they continued steadfastly in the apostles' doctrine and fellowship, in the breaking of bread, and in prayers. Then fear came upon every soul, and many wonders and signs were done through the apostles. Now all who believed were together, and had all things in common, and sold their possessions and goods, and divided them among all, as anyone had need. So continuing daily with one accord in the temple, and breaking bread from house to house, they ate their food with gladness and simplicity of heart, praising God and having favor with all the people. And the Lord added to the church daily those who were being saved.

Acts 2:42-47

4. People are uninvolved. People are uninvolved because they are uncommitted. This completes a tragic, vicious circle. True commitment leads to that free, total involvement discussed in the preceding section. People need a sense of personal identity, of knowing who God truly made them to be. Frequently, they discover their identity because they become associated with some purpose. To find themselves, people find a cause and become committed to that cause. The Church is intended by God to be "the cause," the ultimate and definitive cause above all causes.

When local assemblies fail to inspire and compel commitment to God's cause, people devote their energies to secular substitutes. Charitable societies, service clubs, educational foundations and political and social concerns now exist outside the Church because the Church failed to discharge her Bible-mandated service responsibilities in these areas. Even medical and health organizations, which largely originated from the Church, are popularly conceded to be the sacred domains of government and society at large.

All people commit their lives to something. In reality, "uncommitted Christians" are those who guide and devote their energies and attentions elsewhere, not to the Church. They are building a different kingdom. There are only two life choices that can direct every thought, will, word or action—the service of God or the service of anti-God. Although I stated this in a previous chapter, we would do well to read it again. "Do you not know," asks Paul, "that to whom you present yourselves slaves to obey, you are that one's slaves whom you obey, whether of sin leading to death, or of obedience leading to righteousness?" (Rom. 6:16). The truth is, few Christians really know or believe Paul's words here. Although commitment in service to the Church holds the only true opportunity for lasting and legitimate feelings of identity and security, most Christians elect ignorance or rebellion toward God's great cause.

These four basic problems of leaders and members may be underscored by a single word: mismanagement. Finances are spent unnecessarily and for wrong staffing. Church programs are neglected. Church facilities are poorly maintained. Parts of facilities may be unclean, even unhealthy. It adds up to waste. Everywhere in local churches God's gifts are being wasted. Most tragic are the wasted lives—inspirations, ideas, dreams, potentials, time and resources of people—all unused in expressing the goodness of God. One of the deep distresses I experience as a local church pastor is my grief over men and women who choose to squander their potential and purpose.

The answer—the forgotten, neglected, scorned answer—is servanthood; people who serve.

I say forgotten, neglected and scorned because these words represent the basic rebellion we regularly show our Master. Yet we call Him "Lord."

Priorities are not what people wish them to be; real priorities are what people actually live. If I tell you that my priority is to have daily morning devotions, but do not spend time with the Lord, then I am untrue to you and am only kidding myself. My priority is, in fact, whatever I do in place of daily devotions. If I tell you, "Christ is my Lord," yet practice serving myself, the same pattern holds true.

Who today desires to be a servant when he can be a master? In this age of specialization, spiritual gift distinctives and unique ministries, a person chooses his involvement based on his perception of his individual calling. For self-promotion, self-protection and preservation of uniqueness, people constantly contrast their ministry with those of others. "What is *your* ministry?" is perhaps the question asked most regularly by conference-goers.

If we take an honest look, we find that the underlying motivation of those concerned about "their" ministry is their desire for personal advancement in popularity, recognition, reputation or some combination of these three. Pride reigns as lord above Jesus. For those with this mind-set, the word "servant" conjures up repugnant mental pictures of personal degradation—menial tasks and demeaning duties. But Jesus said, "The Son of Man did not come to be served, but to serve, and to give His life a ransom for many" (Matt. 20:28).

People would like to let it go at that: Let Jesus be the servant and ourselves be His benefactors. They desire the rights and privileges of Christianity with none of its requirements or responsibilites. They are quite willing to abort unrecognized Christian service like a loathed or unwanted pre-born.

It should not be this way. I have grimly described the facts to emphasize how profoundly we need the divine truth of servanthood—believers who truly serve with servants' hearts. Servanthood is not just an alternative; it's the answer. The *only* answer.

Servanthood is people, and people—members of Christ's Body—are the only answer. The Church is God's practical plan for man. Not the government, not society, not the parachurch. The Church is Plan A. There is no back up or contingency plan. There is no Plan B.

> *For I say, through the grace given to me, to everyone who is among you, not to think of himself more highly than he ought to think, but to think soberly, as God has dealt to each one a measure of faith. For as we have many members in one body, but all the members do not have the same function, so we, being many, are one body in Christ, and individually members of one another.*
>
> Romans 12:3-5

Similarly, First Corinthians 12:12-27 thoroughly expresses both the diversity and necessity of each member of the Body. In these two scriptures Paul gives instruction concerning local church interrelational attitudes, framing his remarks in the metaphor of the human body. The problems he describes are the ones I discussed earlier in this chapter: 1) parts that assume responsibility for the whole (the *overworked*); 2) independent parts with no reference to the whole (the *improperly working*); 3) parts unwilling to care for or be involved with other parts (the *uninvolved* or unworking); and 4) parts focused on themselves alone (the *uncommitted* and self-serving).

To answer, Paul frames the solution in the context of a properly functioning body. The answer is the Church, the whole Body of Christ, in which every member contributes, in which the single greatest cause for every member is service, support and supply for the lack of every other member.

Service. Service is through every Body member. Service through every Body member should be accomplished for the sake of every other Body member. This is the only means by which God's people will ever achieve the goal of corporate maturity. Servanthood of Christian members supplying adequacy to fill the lack of other Christian members is Paul's message to the Romans, the Corinthians, the Ephesians and to us.

> *For the equipping of the saints for the work of ministry, for the edifying of the body of Christ, till we all come to the unity of the faith and of the knowledge of the Son of God, to a perfect man, to the measure of the stature of the fullness of Christ; that we should no longer be children, tossed to and fro and carried about with every wind of doctrine, by the trickery of men, in the cunning craftiness of deceitful plotting, but, speaking the truth in love, may grow up in all things into Him who is the head—Christ—from whom the whole body, joined and knit together by what every joint supplies, according to the effective working by which every part does its share, causes growth of the body for the edifying of itself in love.*
>
> Ephesians 4:12-16

None of this is idealistic or theoretical. Paul asserts positively what he knows to be reality. In our own church, we experience some of this same reality because we continue to undergo painful struggles with these same basic problems and sinful attitudes. Because we have struggled and have been willing to attempt what God's Spirit and Word require, we have discovered that it is possible for individuals and churches to fulfill God's intent of servanthood. Not only is it possible, it is instructed, commanded and required. The message of biblical servanthood is true, plausible, practical and achievable—if we are willing to receive it and act upon it.

Servanthood must be taught. People daily express by their behavior what they think, believe and imagine. Literally, they are who they believe they are, and become who they believe they are to become. Solomon said, "For as he thinks in his heart, so is he" (Prov. 23:7).

All ideas, concepts and thoughts have consequences in this life. What a person thinks controls his decisions, actions, feelings and, to a great extent, his circumstances.

If a person believes something is good, right, important, valuable, proper or absolutely essential, then his life will be controlled by it. That is, he will live his life in order to attain it. So whether he does it, has it, gets it or whether it happens to him, it will affect, even determine, the way he lives.

By the same token, if a person believes something is horrible, undesirable, catastrophic, unbearable, unpleasant, repulsive or absolutely hopeless, then it, too, will control his life because he will live in order to avoid it. So then, whether he does it or receives it or whether it happens to him, it will affect and determine the way he lives.

Of supreme importance in local churches, then, is the ministry of worship and the presenting of the Word in a way that confronts and changes our thoughts from the unbiblical to the biblical. That is why servanthood must be taught first. Right teaching confronts wrong thinking.

Certainly, if people believe servanthood is good, right, important, valuable, proper or absolutely essential, then they will speak, choose, live and experience servanthood. On the other hand, if people believe it to be horrible, undesirable, catastrophic, unbearable, unpleasant, repulsive, creating utter hopelessness or limited to those specifically called to ministry or service, then people will tend to avoid it. It all depends on what people believe to be true.

Thus it is necessary for the vision and instruction of biblical servanthood to be a banner continually raised before the people. Servanthood must be taught and retaught in public and in private.

Teaching never becomes unnecessary. I would venture to say that in our congregation, not a meeting goes by in which the subject of servanthood is not in some way included. Certainly this concept is fundamentally and integrally woven into every ministry program we conduct. For when teaching ceases, the influencing mental attention once devoted to servanthood is soon lost. It gets outshouted by the multitude of other thoughts that daily clamor for attention.

The apostle Peter understood this need for repetition and reminder when he promised:

For this reason I will not be negligent to remind you always of these things, though ye know and are established in the present truth. Yes, I think it is right, as long as I am in this tent, to stir you up by reminding you.

II Peter 1:12-13

I am advocating no extraordinary or unusual teaching. Servanthood is not some strange new doctrine. Servanthood is the normal Christian life. But Christian people do not know that. Christian leaders do not know it. So the Church needs to be taught it.

The crucial need is not for challenge, but for change. As others have said, reformation is not what is needed; transformation is. Transformation occurs with genuine repentance: We abandon our thoughts, agree with God's thoughts, receive them as our own and then live accordingly. Teaching—that is, continued presentation of truth and its application to life—is the primary means by which God's thoughts are conveyed. A scripture usually applied to evangelism is equally applicable to servanthood:

> *How then shall they call on Him in whom they have not believed? And how shall they believe in Him of whom they have not heard? And how shall they hear without a preacher?*

> Romans 10:14

How indeed may we call on God to become His true servants if we have no one to hold the Word of truth before us?

Servanthood must be expected. Positive expectancy is the required prevailing attitude. The first attitude on which to work is your own. If your goal is to be a servant, and if you desire to cause others to become servants, then you must decide now to let go of all negative attitudes and excuse-making.

"But you don't know my staff (or my people, or my special problems, or my locality, etc.)."

"It works for you because you have a unique ministry."

"It works for you because you have so many young people."

"My people will never receive the message."

"If we begin to practice servanthood as you say, we would have to restructure every department and program. Our church couldn't handle that."

"It will cause us to become too in-grown. We will neglect other important ministries."

"We are a specialty church. God hasn't called us to servanthood."

Over the years I have heard from leaders dozens of reasons for why servanthood won't work. To state it more honestly, I have heard men and women attempt to justify their choice to not receive the message. The central cause of all failure to pursue God's perfect plan is not "can't" but "won't." "Won't" is usually determined by the work required. The famous excuse, "I'm too busy to get organized" is really another way of saying "I'm too lazy to work more effectively to improve my work efforts."

Repentance, therefore, is essential. To adopt the new, one must forsake the old. Paul states it allegorically:

Cast out the bondwoman and her son, for the son of the bondwoman shall not be heir with the son of the freewoman.

Galatians 4:30

Solomon says it plainly:

He who covers his sins will not prosper, but whoever confesses and forsakes them will have mercy.

Proverbs 28:13

When a person declares that he wants servanthood, but secretly retains old attitudes and excuses, his words are only a cover. Instead, believers should elect to put this sign over the doorway of the mind and heart: "Negative Attitudes: No Admittance. Self-Defenses: No Trespassing."

The people whom we influence and whom we desire to influence read the pages of our attitudes before they ever hear our words. If we do indeed influence them, they are destined to become like the person we truly are. We always disciple who and what we are. Since all servanthood lies first in attitude, negative attitudes must be the first to go.

Once the negatives are forsaken and gone, the fundamental attitude of believers in pursuit of servanthood should be positive. Everything about believers' thoughts, desires, words and actions must say, "Servanthood is of God. It is for me. I will do whatever it takes to receive it, to be a servant and to act on it." There must be a positive embracing of all that servanthood means.

Was it not with this very same kind of energy and attitude that you first accepted the gift of personal forgiveness through Christ? God convinced you of the reality of His good news and gave you enough hope to make the right decision. What is true of the gospel is true of part of the gospel. Servanthood is part of the gospel—just as surely as Jesus said:

Yet it shall not be so among you; but whoever desires to become great among you shall be your servant.

Mark 10:43

The answers to a leader's questions of "How can I get my people involved?" "How can I lead them to commitment without legalism?" lie in the level of the leader's own attitude: his expectation, his inspiration, his enthusiasm and ultimately, in the level his own living is dedicated to the cause of service.

A leader's positive attitude will make the difference for not only him, but also those who follow. Servanthood must be expected. If it is indeed expected, then people will respond to the challenge.

First, though, you must be convinced that God through Christ has made you able to satisfy all requirements of attitude and action to fulfill the lowest service. Then, be a convincer. Challenge every kind of thinking that associates greatness with profession, popularity or possessions. Expect your followers to be great with genuine greatness. When a leader expects great things from God's own people, they will stretch to the necessary commitment and involvement to do great things; to do what Jesus calls the greatest thing, to be servant of all.

Servanthood must be allowed. Servanthood must have a context through which it can be expressed. Then specific opportunities to serve need to be permitted and provided.

The context for servanthood is the community life of the church. I say "community life" when I ought simply to say "life of the church." However, to many people "life of the church" means participation in church services and meetings. That is not what I mean.

By church community I do not refer to only owning a special building in which to practice regular religious activities for several hours in a week. The church community is the "communion of saints." It is the whole local body of Christian people, the Body of Christ. The Church is people—all they are, all they have, everything they do and all that happens to them in one hundred and sixty-eight hours a week.

Many church organizations do not have a community life. They have chosen not to have it, or they simply do not know about it. Believers should not let inadequacies determine God's expectancies. Community life is normal New Testament Christianity. It is the regular and expected outlet for nurture and practice of ordinary Christian service.

In our own local church we have a motto by which we choose to live and identify ourselves. We say we are a "people built together into a meaningful relationship in Christ." We take these words very seriously. They express the covenant we have mutually agreed to enter in order to build deep, lasting and godly, open, honest and transparent relationships among ourselves. To us, "people built together into a meaningful relationship in Christ" means we are a servant people, freely loving and caring for one another based on the grace we each experienced through Jesus. It does not mean that we belong to a club, organization or activity, but rather to Christ and each other.

We emphasize having a strong, vital, "vertical" relationship with the Lord and having strong, vital, "horizontal" relationships with one another. We stress interrelationships that are open, honest and transparent. We reject the enjoyment or toleration of relationships contrary to Matthew, chapters 5 and 18. We do not allow unbiblical choices in daily living. We constantly encourage one another to choose right attitudes and right actions. We often remind each other that if Christianity is anything, it is everything. We believe that every aspect of our life is Christian and completely interrelates with every other aspect, whether natural or spiritual. We strive to be totally committed and totally involved. To expect less is to play church rather than to be the Church.

This is not to say we have not gone through the questioning process. We all have. "But why should I serve?" "George or Sally has more time, so why not ask either of them?" "Are you trying to take advantage of me?" "Do you mean you want me to work for free?" "Why not hire somebody to do it?" These questions are self-oriented and job-oriented. They fail to recognize that service in Christ accomplishes far more than merely getting a job done.

Such attitudes, of course, simply cannot survive very long in a healthy, thriving community of the redeemed. Our relationships are too highly valued and our lives too intricately intertwined. That, after all, is God's intent. His people, united in community life, hold tremendous power for protecting each other from sin and for encouraging each other toward greater righteousness and better demonstration of servanthood. The whole is greater than the sum of its parts.

Thus, the Church—brimming with vitality that comes from genuine Christian community—is God's established context for the expression of servanthood. Now something more is needed. After all, service is work. Service is doing. Servants need to be given something to do. Specific service opportunities need to be provided.

In our church we teach that there are only two groups: those who need help and those who are able to help. All of us belong to both groups at all times. The number of opportunities contained in that sentence is the number of opportunities we have to serve. The possibilities are limitless.

Some of the organized, more formal areas of service involvement in our own church include administration, Bible college, building construction and maintenance, campus outreach, charitable work, community outreach, catechism, home care group leading, children's ministries, Christian day school, counselling, custodial, cooperative day care ministry, evangelism, graphics production and publishing, grounds maintenance, missions, new members' class, convalescent center, radio, vehicle maintenance and worship and arts. All service areas are designed with a two-fold purpose: to meet the needs of the Kingdom and the people within it.

We have nearly 100 percent service involvement by our members, each of whom serve, on the average, in five areas. Experience proves that the benefits of serving far exceed the so-called liabilities. Not infrequently, significant employment promotions are received by our members both in position and income. They attribute their success and growth as employees to the training they receive by serving in the church.

For instance, one young woman who majored in engineering in college had no formal training in drafting in ink. But she did become trained to use technical pens while volunteering her service in our graphics production ministry. From her experience there, she developed a personal portfolio which she then could use to secure two part-time positions in drafting, one in the city planning department and the other at our local state university.

Servanthood must be developed. Training is key. Genesis 14:14 says, "Now when Abram heard that his brother was taken captive, he armed his three hundred and eighteen trained servants who were born in his own house, and went in pursuit as far as Dan." Abram and his servants win the battle. Four essential elements of this fighting team are: 1) they are servants; 2) they are born in Abram's house (we would say, they are committed, involved church members); 3) they are armed or equipped with all the necessary tools to accomplish their mission; and, most importantly of all, 4) they are adequately trained. To be born, trained and equipped servants is to be an effective fighting and serving unit. It is the means by which involvement of every member is realized in the local church.

The possibility of a unified local church force that is like the force of Abram—of one mind, heart and soul, speaking the same word, going the same direction—sounds far-fetched. However, I believe that, because the Bible both presents such a church and commands us to be one, God's plan has to be both reasonable and attainable.

Now I plead with you, brethren, by the name of our Lord Jesus Christ, that you all speak the same thing, and that there be no divisions among you, but that you be perfectly joined together in the same mind and in the same judgment.

I Corinthians 1:10

Fulfill my joy by being like-minded, having the same love, being of one accord, of one mind.

Philippians 2:2

Nevertheless, to the degree that we have already attained, let us walk by the same rule, let us be of the same mind.

Philippians 3:16

The challenge to churches and church leadership is "how." How may we attain such unity of mind, will and purpose? How may we have a people who will do what we do, who know *what* to do, *when* to do it, *where* and *why* and *how* to do it right? How may we build a people who will establish others to do in the same way? The answer is training.

In our church, "every-member-involvement" (EMI) is not optional; but neither does it occur only because it is required and demanded. We have EMI because it is: 1) *taught*; 2) *expected*; 3) *allowed*; and 4) *developed*. We train this concept into our people. It is the normal Christian church life of our congregation.

In the Church, the most valuable resource is people. They are the *only* resource. They are the only *appreciable* resource. People are worth being trained. Training people is certainly more profitable than fund-raising. Training is people-building. Fund-raising in the Church is laying claim to temporal possessions. God lays claim to men's lives, for time and eternity.

I have heard of a relief agency that puts this slogan on their packages: "Give me a fish, and I am hungry tomorrow; teach me to fish, and I am hungry no more." The point is well taken. Building the people of the Church—a long-term project—is of far greater value than saving the church programs from immediate crisis. Appeals for money become unnecessary where a people have been built.

People involved in community and servanthood get excited about building other people. They have the same excitement and enthusiasm to continually transform people in holiness and excellence of service as they do to initially transform people through forgiveness and cleansing from sin. Training people is the fulfillment of the call to do "the work of ministry, for the edifying of the body of Christ." The result is that we mutually come "to a perfect man" (Eph. 4:12-13). People-building is not a role confined to the pastor; every member contributes.

I am not suggesting that development of people or any other part of servanthood is easy or convenient. I am presenting the understanding that servanthood in the Church is right and attainable. But servanthood is like a cathedral. It is not a framed building, nor is it a pre-fabricated modular. Its building takes hard and disciplined labor for a long time. People are built together for eternal purposes, to withstand the test of the ages. With adequate knowledge, training, tools and skills, we all may be building, and we all may be built. All of us may become a "people built together into a meaningful relationship in Christ." With the proper perspective we can stay true to the task (though it outlives us) and glorify God by our attitudes and actions, as the following story illustrates.

"What are you doing down there?" asked one of the simple townsfolk to three at the bottom of a great pit.

"I am digging a ditch," complained the first.

"I am building a wall," answered the second.

"I am building this cathedral to worship the Almighty God of the universe," expressed the third. And he offered his Lord words of thankfulness and praise for the privilege of having a part.

Therefore, whether you eat or drink, or whatever you do, do all to the glory of God.

I Corinthians 10:31

And whatever you do, do it heartily, as to the Lord and not to men.

Colossians 3:23

Further Study for Personal Enrichment

Chapter Five

1. What does Paul say is the role of the leader?

2. How should a pastor's leadership excellence be measured?

3. To whom does the work of ministry belong?

4. Why are people uncommitted?

5. _____ confirms, strengthens and establishes the commitment a believer has made to the Lord in heaven.

6. Cite the only true opportunity for lasting and legitimate feelings of identity and security.

7. State what is lost when lives are wasted in local churches.

8. Describe the underlying motivation of people who talk about "my ministry."

9. In a paragraph, share why it is important to teach servanthood in the local church.

10. Why are the words "servanthood" and "expectancy" linked together? Write your answer in a brief paragraph.

11. In a half-page, describe in your own terms what is meant by "people built together into a meaningful relationship in Christ."

12. What two-fold purpose should be accomplished by service areas?

13. In a page, explain "EMI" and why it should be a part of normal church life.

Chapter Six

Rewards of Service

He who receives a prophet in the name of a prophet shall receive a prophet's reward. And he who receives a righteous man in the name of a righteous man shall receive a righteous man's reward.

Matthew 10:41

The one who receives a servant in the name of Christ is surely destined to enjoy the reward of that service. Rewards come both to the server and to the served. The served, if he receives in Christ's name, is given Christ's reward through the servant. The servant also must receive himself as being a servant of Christ in order to receive his legitimate rewards.

No study of servanthood can be complete without discussing a servant's rewards. Rewards are energizers and motivators. Christians not only obey in service because they are commanded, but also because they are energized to fulfill the responsibility of servanthood according to the significance or impact they anticipate. There are seven rewards for service that I will discuss.

1. The first reward for service is dislike—people will not like you.

If you were of the world, the world would love its own. Yet because you are not of the world, but I chose you out of the world, therefore the world hates you. Remember the word that I said to you, "A servant is not greater than his master." If they persecuted Me, they will also persecute you. If they kept My word, they will keep yours also. But all these things they will do to you for My name's sake, because they do not know Him who sent Me.

John 15:19-21

There are various reasons for this reward. The believer may be too much like Jesus, for example. People do not like that. People can no longer understand that believer. They cannot figure him out. He seems strange and peculiar. So his popularity diminishes due to this changed lifestyle. Before, he was the life of the party; now he will not attend the parties. Of course, the Christian is not to seek to continue his popularity with the world. Of far more importance is being popular with Jesus.

People feel put down by the believer's increased spirituality. They think that he thinks he is holier than they are. He no doubt is—in certain aspects. In other areas they may be holier than he. But people do not want to feel the convicting presence of Jesus in a believer. So, to justify themselves in their own minds, and to excuse themselves from having to change, they find fault in the believer.

Another reason for this reward may be that people are proud. Service given by one requires humility to receive on the part of another. All people enjoy occasions of serving and giving, even if they are infrequent. Few enjoy being needy enough to receive. Believer-servants are not threatened by that. They know they have the genuine goods to give to those who are humble and in need. They themselves are not too proud to receive humbly of another's care.

Often a believer's increased attention to the Lord decreases the amount of attention he gives to those closest to him. Also correlated is their loss of control over him as he submits to Christ's control. When a believer ceases to meet the needs of controlling friends and relatives, they feel the loss deeply. They say or think, "I used to be important to you, but now I am not. All you can talk about now is your Jesus!"

"People will not like you." Even this reward can be an energizer. Persecuted saints of the New Testament rejoiced in the simple fact that they had been counted worthy by God to suffer on the behalf of Christ (Acts 5:41). The impact of this reward is eternal only, never temporal.

2. A second reward is that you will enjoy the personal Presence of Jesus.

> *If anyone serves Me, let him follow Me; and where I am, there My servant will be also. If anyone serves Me, him My Father will honor.*

John 12:26

There is no higher blessing than to experience the sweet, intimate presence of the Lord of heaven. Some feel they have it without having had to obey. That is not true. They cannot actually experience fullness of this relationship without obedience, because disobedience is sin and separates from God. Only to the servant belong the words of Christ, "Well done, good and faithful servant." Certainly this kind of intimacy creates much energy for continuing in obedient service.

3. A third reward is personal assurance of sonship.

You are no longer a slave but a son, and if a son, then an heir of God through Christ.

Galatians 4:7

One matures through servanthood into sonship. Sonship is not always pleasant; it involves chastening. "If you endure chastening, God deals with you as sons" (Heb. 12:7). Those who experience the correcting hand of their heavenly Father can be confidently assured that they are loved and that their adjustment relates to growth. Sonship is confirmed to the believer whom God does not allow to go his own way.

Chastening proves sonship, but it is not the only proof. Servanthood also proves sonship. The one who is sure of his role as a servant is likewise secure in his placement as a son. It is a security that creates energy for continued service and sonship.

4. A fourth reward is that of dynamic importance to the Body of Christ. The role of each servant is vital in the building up of the saints. No one else can fulfill his purpose in the unique way that God has designed for him.

But now God has set the members, each one of them, in the body just as He pleased. And the eye cannot say to the hand, "I have no need of you"; nor again the head to the feet, "I have no need of you." No, much rather, those members of the body which seem to be weaker are necessary.

I Corinthians 12:18, 21-22

Christians need each other. Every human body part or member needs every other human body member in order for a human being to be fully capable and fully functioning. Believers have the same relationship. God designed individual parts to be incomplete and inadequate by themselves. He is bringing to full stature a *corporate* man. Every member is necessary. Every member serving in his uniquely created place is necessary because the Body as a whole is of supreme importance. I know of no greater energy or exhilaration than that which comes to one satisfied in his place of serving in Christ's Body.

5. A fifth reward is a leadership role. Servanthood naturally leads to a role of leadership—perhaps not to great position, but to leadership. Because the servant is under authority, a servant has authority.

> *Yet it shall not be so among you; but whoever desires to become great among you shall be your servant.*
>
> Mark 10:43

> *Then Jesus answered and said to them, "Most assuredly, I say to you, the Son can do nothing of Himself, but what He sees the Father do; for whatever He does, the Son also does in like manner."*
>
> John 5:19

Servants are to be leaders in what they have been given to do. A servant who is not a leader is a dupe, a robot or a drone. He has no initiative. He waits to be told. A leader who is not a servant, who is without a servant's heart, is a despot. He is selfish, heartless and cruel in his dealings.

A servant who is a leader is mindful. He is quick to anticipate the need of both his superiors and his subordinates. He lives and leads to serve them both, that both should achieve their fullest potential.

6. A sixth reward is status received, based on relationship with the Master. Even a bondslave (*doulos*, servant) enjoys a position of status, just as Roman bondmen were held in honor as personal slaves of a nobleman or of the emperor. Christians serve the Emperor of all the universe.

If anyone serves Me, him My Father will honor.

John 12:26

Jesus said to him, "If you want to be perfect, go, sell what you have and give to the poor, and you will have treasure in heaven; and come, follow Me." ... So Jesus said to them, "Assuredly I say to you, that in the regeneration, when the Son of Man sits on the throne of His glory, you who have followed Me will also sit on twelve thrones, judging the twelve tribes of Israel.

Matthew 19:21, 28

Although it draws persecution, status as a believer-servant does command respect. The world mocks those who easily are seen as hypocrites. The world shows more appreciation and respect for those who truly live the Christian life, although they may not give them the usual worldly respect. A servant of Christ knows his standing before his Lord. He has nothing to prove. He has nothing to promote. He is energized by the sheer privilege of serving where God has placed him. As he qualifies in secret and as he qualifies in service, he is promoted by the Lord in His own way in honor and authority.

7. A seventh reward is the meeting of the servant's needs. It is the responsibility of all masters to look after the needs of their slaves. Masters feed, house, clothe, protect and bring both material and non-material increase to their servants. Christianity costs everything. It cost Jesus everything. It costs believers everything, yet all is gained through His redemptive love.

And my God shall supply all your need according to His riches in glory by Christ Jesus.

Philippians 4:19

This verse is spoken often to claim its promise. It cannot, however, stand alone. It is attached to a conditional:

Indeed I have all and abound. I am full, having received from Epaphroditus the things sent from you, a sweet-smelling aroma, an acceptable sacrifice, well pleasing to God.

Philippians 4:18

The Philippians had given sacrificially to Paul. They had served him with a gift. Paul was touched by their sacrifice, and he had an inner witness that God had received their gift as an acceptable offering. After acknowledging the quality of their service, Paul goes on to speak over them the promise of Christ's provision, to supply all their need.

Christ gave all. His giving empowers Christians to give. "We love Him, because He first loved us" (I John 4:19). The Philippians gave to Paul according to the gift they received from Christ. Because the Philippians so gave, God was further released to give of Himself. It is a blessed cycle, a holy whirlwind to heaven that ought never to be interrupted. Christian servants cannot *outgive* God, but they should never cease trying to do so.

God does not intend that His servants be mismanaged or discouraged. Servanthood requires all of the servant, but the servant receives in exchange all the rewards God gives for faithful service in His Kingdom.

Further Study for Personal Enrichment

Chapter Six

1. Rewards are _____ and _____ .

2. List the seven rewards of service.

3. In a paragraph, express the delight you received from the rewards with which you have been blessed because of the servanthood expressed through your own life.

4. Servanthood requires _____ of the servant, but the servant receives in exchange all the _____ God gives for _____ service in His Kingdom.

5. Which reward do you like most? Which reward do you like least? Explain your answers in a half-page.

Chapter Seven

Service in
the Local Church

The preceding chapters presented the vision and necessity of Christian servanthood, especially as viewed from the required context of the local church. What remains to be explained is "how." How may a leader effectively transfer the spirit and substance of servanthood into the heart and life of the people he leads?

This question has two answers.

One answer is to have an effective service program. An effective program of service should be sought, taught, understood and applied. As it is implemented, it ought then to be adapted and developed according to the specific needs and make-up of one's local church: its particular people, its corporate calling, its unique locale. The majority of this chapter deals with the explanation of the service program.

However, another answer must be considered first; one that goes beyond the essential of having an adequate program, one that is more serious, is of greater urgency and needs priority attention.

That answer is the servanthood of the leader.

THE LEADER AND HIS SERVICE

Let a leader examine himself. Let him seriously scrutinize his own soul. Let him compare himself to his Christ. Does he serve with Christ's service? Does he serve with His heart? For as a leader serves, so does he lead. He influences others to serve only to the extent that he himself serves with a servant's heart.

The influencing leader may teach all that he knows, but he will also disciple and impart who and what he is. It is improbable for him to lead beyond the limits of his own knowledge, experience and condition. "The disciple is not above his master," Jesus said. "Everyone who is perfectly trained will be like his teacher" (Luke 6:40). A leader cannot expect his people to serve unless he himself is a servant.

Therefore, the leader himself must be convinced and committed to the servanthood message. It is not enough to read about it in a book. It is not enough to become enthused over the possibility of having a serving congregation. It is not enough to implement even the best of service programs. Full, personal commitment to the message and life of service is required of the leader. The leader must live and move and have his being in Christ's servanthood. Jesus challenged His disciples, "Are you able to drink the cup that I am about to drink, and be baptized with the baptism that I am baptized with?" (Matt. 20:22). So the leader himself must be ready, willing, able and active in an immersion of the servant's life.

Such baptism in service requires the leader's all: his life, talents, goals, dreams, aspirations, vision, future, money, ideas, family, education and so on. "Let goods and kindred go," wrote Luther, "this mortal life, also."[1] Paul said as much: "For to me, to live is Christ" (Phil. 1:21). He could say, I exist to be Christ's servant because I exist to be your servant. "For we do not preach ourselves, but Christ Jesus the Lord, and ourselves your bond-servants for Jesus' sake" (II Cor. 4:5). "Inasmuch as you did it to one of the least of these My brethren, you did it to Me" (Matt. 25:40).

Servanthood is instilled in that leader who is willing to be discipled in servanthood. "Train up a child in the way he should go" (Prov. 22:6). The way that the Christian leader should go is the way of servanthood. The developing leader disciplines his own soul. By the help of the Holy Spirit he trains himself in the way he should go; he masters his own inner man. The resulting, actual maturity proves the effectiveness of the personal discipling process. In authentic maturity, the soul does not depart from the path of its disciplined training.

This is the concept of discipleship, or disciplined training, that was used by the Lord Jesus. *Everyone who is perfectly trained will be like his teacher.* Christ intensively trained the twelve so that they would be like Him.

Notice the process Jesus used. First, He taught and demonstrated the gospel right in front of them. He made His disciples watch. Then, at a time of His choosing, the roles reversed. Recall that He sent them on their own missions journeys, especially two by two. His followers were put to practice, and He watched and evaluated.

1.　Luther, Martin, "A Mighty Fortress Is Our God," translated by F.H. Hedge, printed in *Tabernacle Hymns Number Five*, Tabernacle Publishing Company, Chicageo, 1953 (1969 Printing).

At the end of the process, the protégé becomes like his mentor in thought, word and deed. The philosophies, ideals, spirit and skills of the leader are transferred and replicated. All who are perfectly developed in serving will become like the servant in their leader. The more intensively that leader is committed to the cause of servanthood in his church, the more his soul will be transferred by word and deed to the soul of those who follow him.

SERVICE PROGRAMS

If servanthood is the personal lifestyle of the leader, then it surely can and will be established in the corporate Christian community through an appropriate service program. Having an appropriate and effective program of service provides a channel for this process. Servanthood is the end; the service program is the means. It is the *how-to*.

The principles that follow are principles of *how-to*. They have been, and still are, highly productive and useful in our church. They have undergone years of testing, proving and refinement. They are biblical. *They work for us by helping us to efficiently and effectively emulate Christ and implement His purposes. I believe they will work for you.*

1. Teach God's perspective on servanthood in the local church. There is no time when a pastor can cease sharing with his people the vision God has given him, especially the vision of servanthood. No doubt the vision will expand. No doubt God will add elements to its fundamental contents—just as surely as He adds people to His Church daily and increases her resources. But to cease teaching the servanthood vision is to induce the Church to cease her cause.

"Where there is no revelation, the people cast off restraint" Solomon says (Prov. 29:18). Hosea prophesies, "My people are destroyed for lack of knowledge" (Hos. 4:6). What vision? What knowledge? People need to *see* where they are going. People need a constant reminder of their purpose. Otherwise they give up. They lose heart. If their own leader does not press them in the cause, they soon slip away to a new leader and a new cause.

In this sense the local church pastor is ever God's prophet to His people. God has a specific message for a specific people in a definite time and place in order to lead them in a distinct direction. Responsibility for clear declaration is the pastor's.

A leader must ever recall to his people's attention the word of service. Jesus did. The necessity of service is a message Jesus continually presented. He inspired, urged and even required service. He required it in action, and He required it in heart. The chief attribute of all greatness, He said, is ability and evidence of serving all (Matt. 23:11).

So, the leader must follow Christ in charging the servant's duties. He should exhort in sermons and teachings, at every opportunity, both in public and in private. He should encourage, instruct and challenge. He should speak in general terms, yet address himself very specifically to those who ought to hear. He should call for repentance. Repentance unto service should be preached because people need to know how to change. The vision of service should be preached, because people need to understand and appreciate what they are to become.

Servanthood as a subset of the gospel is to be offered and enjoined in the same way as the gospel itself: through enlightenment, agreement, repentance and prayer. Ultimately, each individual must know that he has actually spiritually progressed in the servanthood vision. He returns from the altar assured that he is a different person—more conformed to Him who lays down His life in service. Just as repentance is an ongoing experience in life, so is recommitment to servanthood an ongoing experience throughout life.

My own experience teaches that exhortation to the vision of servanthood flows very naturally in the worship service. Because of our now inherent commitment to the servanthood message and practice at our church, the topic finds its place in nearly every sermon and discussion.

Incidentally, it is not by chance that the Church uses the words "worship services" to label her gatherings. Without question worship is service, and service is worship. But unfortunately for many who attend weekly worship services, that is where their servanthood ends. Instead, servanthood should have its very beginning in regular worship.

2. Understand and teach God's specific vision for service. God provides each pastor with an awareness and burden for his own people's service opportunities. At all times he is Christ's herald of Christ's specific vision for his local church. Not every congregation is the same. Not every location is the same. Therefore, specific service opportunities and needs are as diverse as personalities and demographics.

Of course, general service responsibilities of the Church are universal. Facilities need to be cleaned, repaired and maintained. Visitors need to be hosted. The troubled need to be heard and the bereaved comforted. The sick need to be visited. The poor need to be provided with goods. The Word needs to be preached. Unbelievers need to be evangelized and baptized. Believers need to be instructed, catechized, established and confirmed, both in faith and in life. Many leaders have learned to implement and use delegated ministry through small care groups and other means; except, I have often found, without first establishing proper attitudes in their delegates' hearts.

The specific *how-to* vision and burden from God are as unique as the local church itself. I believe that the senior pastor is to be the vision-setter and doctrine-establisher of the local expression of Christ's Body. With him lies the final responsibility to receive from the Lord and to solidly fix in his people specific applications of the servanthood vision. Some areas he ought to consider include the following list, and every other ministry area appropriate to his congregation. These are service areas in which our church is involved as a local congregation.

Adult Christian education, adult Sunday school
Bible college ministry
Bible studies, prayer, fellowship groups
Career planning, employment skills, employment services
Catechism ministry
Charitable causes and social services
Children's education, Christian day school
Children's ministries, Sunday school
Christian day care
Church administration, governmental ministry, deacons, elders
Church planting
Church/home construction, maintenance, repair

Church/home grounds, landscaping
Counseling: domestic, financial, singles, substance
    abuse, etc.
Custodial ministry
Dramatic arts
Emergency care, used clothing
Evangelism, community outreach
Exhortation, preaching ministry
Fine arts, crafts
Giving
Healing, spiritual gifts
Home group or cell groups, ministry to families
Hospital ministry
Hospitality
Intercession
Ministry to convalescents and shut-ins
Ministry to young marrieds
Missions
Motivation, encouragement
New members' class
Personal care
Prophetic ministry
Shepherding
Singles ministry
Teaching ministry
Time management, scheduling, self-discipline
Vehicle care, maintenance, repair
Weddings and receptions
Worship, music
Youth ministry, college-age ministry

Many of these ministry areas deal with the intrinsic
care of a church. People have difficulty with this because

they were so thoroughly taught the concepts of outreach and charity. Yet, the fact is, a church that is not internally strong and maintained cannot strongly reach out. Ephesians 4:11-16 powerfully declares this, ending with, "cause growth of the body for the edifying of *itself* in love" (emphasis added).

If you are a pastor considering this list for your own congregation, you should ask these hard questions and write down the answers you believe are from the Lord: "Where do I begin?" "What are the specific ministry areas God would have for my local church?" "What is the priority of these ministries?" "Am I responding to the desire of the people or to the direction God has shown me?" "What do I do that my people should do instead?" "What is it that only I can do?" "How may I begin to establish the work of service?" "In whom shall I begin the process?"

As you proceed to implement new opportunities of servanthood, you should remember to go slowly, exercising care and caution. Advance in order of the highest priority which has easier capabilities of teaching and establishing servanthood, and have full support from your local church governing board.

It is no shame to go to work on only one or a few areas. "Who has despised the day of small things?" (Zech. 4:10). At all times the leader is building first a people, not just a ministry. Great *esprit de corps* is evident among those whose souls are mustered by a leader for the same cause. Therefore, your attention as pastor should be focused specifically on the ministry equipment most needed by your people. In this manner all servants in the group "go through the same door," the door of disciplined training by you, their local church shepherd. All become trained in one mind, one heart, one judgment and one commitment, so that all speak the same word.

Remember that the primary goal of this process is not the meeting of needs. The primary goal is building an equipped, serving Christian people, perfected as Christ in heart, mind and action. With fixed attention on the primary goal of building and equipping a unified serving people, the secondary goal of meeting actual needs will indeed also be fulfilled.

3. Consider the location where service will take place. Rural ministry is not the same as urban ministry. Neither is it the same as ministry in the suburbs. Not every "rural" area is the same; neither is every "urban" area or every "suburban" area. Each has its peculiar social structures. Service opportunities, needs and responsibilities are distinct in every case. You as pastor must be spiritually and socially attuned to the geographical setting to which you have been called. You must rally, train and equip your assembly to serve accordingly.

Consider, for example, the ministry of missions. Typically, a local congregation meets the responsibility of missions work in one or both of two ways: 1) it sends financial or other support to a missions organization, either that of the denomination or an independent agency, and 2) it sends financial or other support to a specific missionary or missionaries. Both of these are legitimate ways in which to serve the Lord in the area of missions. Direct involvement is unusual.

However, the specific location of our own congregation has influenced us to be more directly involved. This region, called the Palouse Empire, is a golden harvest for world missions. Students from around the globe arrive annually for higher education and career training at any of four area colleges or universities. A number have discovered, to their surprise, that the Lord has called them to a higher service. Thus, missions dollars and missions workers from our church are committed to the campus outreach programs of our own locale. The congregation knows worldwide impact simply because of its faithful commitment to serve in this region.

Moreover, world exposure at the local level has opened our eyes to the opportunity of inviting from other countries people interested in intensive and specialized ministry training. Our own church's missions pastors, a husband and wife, directly oversee a rigorous nine-month development program for incoming internationals. These pastors also conduct short-term missions tours to other nations for our members.

In addition, individuals from our own ranks have been called and prepared for Christian service on the foreign field. One woman serves in East Africa, working to establish a church while she teaches at the Makerere University.

The sort of direct missions involvement that our church presently enjoys likely would not have come about had we not fully given ourselves in service to our own unique region with its academic emphasis. God has given every church its own unique region of ministry.

4. Consider the people who will serve and use wisdom in setting them into their places. In his letters to Timothy and Titus, Paul particularly addresses himself to the roles of bishop, or elder, and deacon in the local church. However, general principles drawn from his comments establish certain principles for all service areas: 1) positions of service have specific titles by which they are recognized and distinguished; 2) positions of service have definite qualifications; and 3) positions of service have certain responsibilities, or job descriptions. If a person fails to meet the necessary qualifications or fails to adequately perform responsibilities, he disqualifies himself from the service area. Thus a leader should give careful attention to evaluating people who will serve in light of the requirements of service.

Consider natural qualifications. What are the natural and developed skills of those who will serve? Are they appropriate to the area of service? Natural qualifications are part of the overall equation, but their absence does not necessarily disqualify people from service in a particular area. Frequently, specific service is a means of gaining experience, training and skills.

Consider moral qualifications. Roles of service in a church are on a continuum. All members of the church should serve, but each has a different level of Christian maturity. Not all servanthood is equal. Various roles of service require various levels of maturity. Certainly increased responsibility needs increased personal integrity and exemplary living. Is the lifestyle of the person commensurate to the position of service? Does it enhance and contribute to that service? Does the person have a reputation for honesty and integrity both in his church and in the world?

Consider the style and personality of the one who will serve. Is he engaging, inspiring and enthusiastic? Is he driven, commanding and accomplishing? Is he principled, methodical and orderly? Or is he easy-going, friendly and cooperative? Generally speaking, the role of service ought to be suitable to that person's style. If not, the leader must know what God, through service, is seeking to effect in that one's life.

Most importantly, *consider a person's spiritual qualifications*. These include the quality and consistency of his personal relationship with Jesus. Does he experience intimate communion with Christ on a daily basis? Does he read his Bible daily? Does he worship and pray daily? Does he listen to what God says? Does he obey?

Other spiritual essentials include the quality and consistency of that person's relationship with his church—especially with those who oversee him. Is he open, honest and transparent? Does he share freely and vulnerably about matters of sin and personal failure, about matters of conviction and personal holiness? Will he confess his sin when he knows his exposure may cause self-disqualification from continued service?

Spiritual criterion for service also includes the two key traits of loyalty and faithfulness. David poses the question, "Who may abide in Your tabernacle? Who may dwell in Your holy hill?" Then he answers in part, "He honors those who fear the LORD; He who swears to his own hurt and does not change" (Ps. 15:1, 4). Certainly David's words embrace the character quality of loyalty. Who will swear in commitment, and not turn away from the commitment he has made? Find that person. Involve him in service. He is loyal.

Faithfulness is a second key. Recall the three things in which servants are to be found faithful: 1) in that which is least; 2) in matters of money; and 3) in that which belongs to another. Carefully evaluate the faithfulness of your own local church servants by these three standards.

On these bases, leaders are to prove and approve their people for roles of specific service. Paul says, "Let these also first be tested; then let them serve" (I Tim. 3:10). When a would-be servant is carefully and honestly evaluated by his godly leader, according to natural skill and knowledge, morality and lifestyle, propriety of personality and spiritual maturity, then that person can be given, with confidence, suitable responsibilities.

On proving growth and sanctification in these qualifying areas, he also may be appropriately promoted as the Lord leads.

In this way the leader serves as God's hands extended to fulfill the scripture that says, "Exaltation comes neither from the east nor from the west nor from the south. But God is the Judge: He puts down one, and exalts another" (Ps. 75:6-7). In all things we should recognize what God is doing, rather than just organizing to get the job done. *Too much of church work is done by those who reluctantly volunteer or who cannot say no; spiritual qualification is not considered.*

In the matter of promotion, please remember two cautions. First, promotion does not need to be to a so-called higher position. I am not in favor of creating a hierarchy of service assignments in the local church. Too often members are taught to strive toward assignments inappropriately judged to be higher or more honored. The idea is against the very spirit of servanthood. Any person duly gifted by God for a particular task should feel profound personal contentment in serving in that area, no matter how "insignificant," and with no internal or external pressure of desiring something more or "advancing up the ladder."

Paul commands that "whatever you do, do it heartily, as to the Lord" (Col. 3:23). Promotion from the Lord is predominantly spiritual and therefore felt spiritually by the recipient. Thus, the leaders who are instruments to minister tangible spiritual promotion should not overlook or ignore the work of those who seldom make the spotlight. Certainly they should be deeply appreciated and be encouraged for their labor, their product and their contentment. On the other hand, all Christians should serve because they are Christians and not because they are motivated by recognition. Christians are servants who receive eternal rewards, not easy and corruptible, temporal crowns.

Second, it is character and faithfulness that primarily should be rewarded, not talent. Never promote on the basis of talent alone. Why? Talent, like knowledge, "puffs up." All talents are graces received to be properly used. They do not indicate that one Christian is in some way better or more blessed than another. Pride has no place in servanthood. These two characteristics are mutually exclusive and are contradictory.

This kind of estimation or judgment of church members is not easy. It requires the leader himself to squarely face his God and give an account of his own qualifications to serve. But for him who, in the interest of servanthood, will be true first to honest self-judgment and then to honest evaluation of his members, something remarkable will occur. God will raise up for that leader a committed, loyal, serving team. Where once the pastor did everything by himself, he will have now reproduced himself in the lives of a few. They in turn will do the same, and God's plan of multiplication of ministry will be effected.

5. Create an administrative structure for each service area. Create an overall structure for all areas. Define successive tiers of responsibility. Map them out on charts. Designate each specific role. Show how various roles of service are intended to relate to other roles.

A structure chart is like the layout of furniture in a home. Though occasionally pieces are added or replaced, a family's furniture generally remains the same. But, that furniture can be moved about as often as desired for the overall accommodation of the owner, family and guests. Moving the furniture can change the appearance, function and usefulness of a room entirely.

In the same way that a home has furniture, every service area in the church must have defined and flexible structure. That structure does not have to be perfect. It is to change as often as necessary in order to continue progressing in the overall vision of that church. To put it another way, "perfection" of structure is what the leader determines, under God's guidance, for a particular, limited time. Structure ceases to be perfect when it no longer represents or serves the administrated area of service.

Defined structure is important for two reasons. One reason concerns the issue of authority and responsibility. Structure establishes a clear chain of authority and responsibility. Every team member knows where he stands. His responsibilities have been defined with certainty by the superior who commissioned him. The servant is confident that for every assigned duty, he has commensurate authority, so he freely goes about his tasks. He has authority because he is under authority. In this way structure creates security for the servant, and security promotes his success.

The second issue is that of communication. Defined structure sets up the flow for information and reporting: downward, upward and laterally. The vision and heart of servanthood, specific directions for serving, needed encouragement, adjustment, correction, rebuke—these are communicated downward. Feedback, reports, questions, concerns, distresses or particular difficulties of serving are communicated upward. Laterally, servants communicate encouragement, support, confidence and motivation to all of their teammates. Clean, open and properly functioning lines of communication are paramount. Where open and honest communication is not actively encouraged and practiced, confusion, tension, strife, bitterness, complaint, envy and rivalry can be rife in any department, either in potential or in blatant practice.

Let me say a final word about created structure. Lateral or adjunct positions are to be recognized. However, take care that two or more positions do not share identical responsibilities. A department should not have two heads. If two authorities are necessary, clear distinctions of responsibility should be defined and clear lines of communication established. In this way confusion is averted. At all times a leader should know who his followers are, and servants should know who is their head.

6. Write down the vision and description for the service areas. Train servants according to what is written. The Lord commanded Habakkuk to "Write the vision, and make it plain on tablets, that he may run who reads it" (Hab. 2:2). A plainly written statement of vision and of mission is fuel for intense and wholehearted serving. Write it plainly, and local church servants will zealously run with it.

I recommend that a leader write his description for service in the form of a service manual. Typically, service manuals have at least four parts: 1) a structure chart for the area (additional charts may be necessary to show how this area relates to other departments); 2) a clear communication of overall vision and heart for the service; 3) job descriptions; and 4) directions for specific tasks. All four parts are necessary. All are vital. Structure charts and vision statements are crucial. Job descriptions and specific directions are equally imperative.

Job descriptions are the vision and mission statement for each individual servant. The heart of servanthood for that particular role is defined and set into words. Job descriptions—indeed the manuals themselves—are more than an outline of rules and regulations. They are heart communication in respect to the minutest details. In job descriptions specific duties are clearly stated, of course. But a proper service manual never misses an opportunity to reinforce the heart of servanthood.

Specific directions for tasks are likewise a necessary part of any manual. God in His Church is concerned not only with what service is performed, but also with how it is done. Excellence is the trademark of all that He does. It is said of Jesus, the individual, "He has done all things well"—with excellence and distinction (Mark 7:37). The corporate Jesus, the Church, should have the same reputation. The world berates the Church for not living up to her claims, and much of the criticism is deserved. She is not without power to conduct herself with nobility. He has provided His Word and His Spirit. Written directions for tasks of service are a direct and immediate local church application of the Word and Spirit He has provided.

Throughout the manual, thoughts should be set down in clear, concise, understandable and definite terms. Do the words have to be perfect? Does the manual itself have to be perfect? Only as perfect as the leader determines in order to accurately, faithfully and with excellence communicate servanthood—its vision and application—to his own local church.

Manuals should be written with three questions in mind: "How is this area of service functioning in my church at the present time?" "How is this service area supposed to function?" "How can this area of service grow to remain productive as the church grows or changes?" Search the Scriptures for precepts and examples of servanthood application. Review the service manual regularly and revise it according to progressive illumination from the Word and from experience. In this sense a manual for service is never fully written. There are always further ways to "go on to perfection."

Service manuals are instruments for instruction. They are training manuals. They represent the vision and method of servanthood that God has given a pastor for his own local church. Those who teach from service manuals are reinforcers of their pastor's vision. Moreover, service manuals can be used to instruct members in the pastor's recommended principles of administration, management and leadership. Enrichment and improvement of the whole serving team is the overall result.

In our congregation, we regularly present training workshops conducted from service manuals. Normally, workshops are presented on an annual basis. Individuals involved in service areas are urged to read the appropriate manuals on their own also. Some are expected to review the contents quarterly. The purpose is to keep the vision of servanthood constantly before the servers, and to maintain excellence of heart and action for corporate expression of the life of Christ.

Insofar as they are taught, read and heeded, service manuals ensure a servant's success. Everyone loves to succeed. Service manuals guarantee success. Manuals are a pattern, or blueprint, for specific serving. They are written instructions for a contained, fail-proof system. Individuals who serve "according to the book" know exactly what is expected, when and how. They know where to go for answers and for assistance. Individuals succeed in service because they follow the vision set forth by the pastor in the pages of the service manual. Individuals succeed, the team succeeds, the whole church body succeeds and is built up. More than a job gets accomplished. Success breeds success, and lives are eternally changed because of the servanthood spirit.

7. Regularly evaluate the service team. Feedback, communication and knowledge of an individual's applied response to service is as important as the message of servanthood itself. Paul said, "I bear in my body the marks of the Lord Jesus" (Gal. 6:17). What are Jesus' marks? They are evidence of His suffering and persecution. But why did Paul suffer? "Now if we are afflicted," he said, "it is for your consolation and salvation" (II Cor. 1:6). He also stated, "Who now rejoice in my sufferings for you, and fill up that which is behind of the afflictions of Christ in my flesh for his body's sake, which is the church" (Col. 1:24, KJV). Certainly suffering is not the only evidence of servanthood. But Paul's point is well taken. He devoted his life to the servanthood cause. Marks of his service may readily be known.

"Iron sharpens iron" (Prov. 27:17), and Christ has ordained His Church as the instrument of her own sanctification. When in Christ every serving member is "joined and knit together by what every joint supplies," when there is "effective working by which every part does its share," then there can be full "growth of the body for the edifying of itself in love" (Eph. 4:16). Evaluation of servanthood is a part of the sanctifying process. It is a way of knowing the effective working of every part.

Christ has ordained His ascension gift ministries and the pastor in particular to be evaluators of the flock of God. "Be diligent to know the state of your flocks," commands Solomon, "and attend to your herds" (Prov. 27:23). How else will God's leaders fulfill their role as equippers of saints for ministry to edify Christ's Body? Responsibility to equip requires recognizing need or lack among the saints. It presupposes careful evaluation of that lack in order to correctly fill it. Evaluation of service may require that responsibilities be added to the one who serves. It may require that responsibilities be taken away. But it is surely intended to accomplish two things: 1) improvement of the individual's servant's heart and service duties and 2) improvement of the heart and function of the whole serving team.

Confidentiality of records is to be maintained always. All in the chain who read or write service evaluations should be taught to handle information with utmost discretion, respect and care. Theirs is a sacred trust. They are acting directly on behalf of the local church shepherd himself. They receive and communicate only to those necessary and to no one else. Recall the example of the gentleman's gentleman. To expose, embarrass or in any way shame his master, even by accident, would be reprehensible, villainous and unthinkable. The same attitude should be found in the one who evaluates or who reads evaluations, for they are held in the same trust.

NOTE: In conjunction with the preceding discussion, please see the Appendix for the following examples: 1) a line-authority diagram of a specific service crew traced through the structure of a local church; 2) contents of a service manual; 3) a job description from a service manual; and 4) two methods for evaluating service—one for crew members and one for crew leaders or supervisors. For an example of a specific vision statement from a service manual, please see Chapter Two, page 23.

Further Study for Personal Enrichment

Chapter Seven

1. In what two ways may a leader effectively transfer the spirit and substance of servanthood into the hearts and lives of the people he leads?

2. What does the influencing leader actually disciple and impart? What does a leader need to be, in order to expect his people to serve?

3. Cite the requirement of the leader if he indeed wants baptism in service.

4. List the seven steps the leader will need to take to establish servanthood in his church.

5. Who is to be the vision-setter and doctrine-establisher of the local expression of Christ's Body?

6. If you are a pastor, prayerfully consider and, in a page, answer all the "hard questions" under point two (page 120): "Understand and teach God's specific vision for service."

7. Which is more important: to build a people or to build a ministry?

8. State the primary goal of this building process.

9. List the three principles of establishing service areas.

10. The leader should consider several areas for evaluating people as he places them into service. Identify these areas of consideration.

11. In light of the material on loyalty and faithfulness, examine yourself and write a prayer asking the Holy Spirit to show you what you need to do to become a more faithful, loyal servant in your local expression of the Body of Christ.

12. From whom does promotion come? What makes a person qualify for promotion?

13. There must be a _____ and _____ structure for every service area in the church.

14. Restate the two reasons defined structure is important.

15. Name the four parts of a service manual.

16. Why should service manuals be constantly reviewed?

17. Whom has Christ ordained to be the particular evaluator of the flock of God?

Chapter Eight

The Heart of a Servant

Christianity is not a one-time experience of justification by faith. Personal salvation, as taught by Paul, is past, present and future. Jesus "delivered us from so great a death," Paul says, "and does deliver us; in whom we trust that He will still deliver us" (II Cor. 1:10). Present deliverance from sin is proof of past forgiveness. Present deliverance is called sanctification. It is a progressive continuation in the faith of Christ. The Bible has many warnings to show that Christianity is to be ongoing:

Therefore consider the goodness and severity of God: on those who fell, severity; but toward you, goodness, if you continue in His goodness. Otherwise you also will be cut off.

Romans 11:22 (Emphasis added.)

And you, who once were alienated and enemies in your mind by wicked works, yet now He has reconciled in the body of His flesh through death, to present you holy, and blameless, and above reproach in His sight: if indeed you continue in the faith, grounded and steadfast, and are not moved away from the hope of the gospel which

you heard, which was preached to every creature under heaven, of which I, Paul, became a minister.
                    Colossians 1:21-23 (Emphasis added.)

We have become partakers of Christ if we hold the beginning of our confidence steadfast to the end.
                    Hebrews 3:14 (Emphasis added.)

"Once saved, always saved" supplies a measure of security perhaps, but in no way does it represent Christian reality. For it is not he who begins who is saved, but he who endures to the end (Matt. 24:13). Obedience to receive the faith and grace of Christ begins the Christian life; progressive obedience according to the progressive revelation of the Spirit causes life to continue. Resolute disobedience can put an end to it.

In these pages I have spoken frequently of a servant's heart. That is because of the questions pastors have asked: "How can I get my people involved?" "How much can I expect from them?" "How can I inspire my people to commitment and service without being demanding or controlling?" The answer is to see that change is effected not only on the outside, but also on the inside. The answer is a servant's heart.

The importance of having a servant's heart cannot be overstated. The work of service not originating from a heart of service is of no eternal value. "The flesh profits nothing" (John 6:63). It may not be harmful, but it assuredly will not be helpful. At best it is a tangential move from God's intended purpose. At worst, it results in actual spiritual injury because service not from a servant's heart may be disobedient interference with God.

I believe that receiving a servant's heart is fundamentally necessary to the Christian experience. Certainly it is necessary for all of servanthood. There can be no true service without a heart to truly serve. The Bible teaches that faithfulness is required of stewards or servants (I Cor. 4:1), but the reverse is true also. The faithful are required to have servants' hearts; it is impossible for a Christian to be faithful without a servant's heart.

What, indeed, is a servant's heart? It is an attitude of serving that permeates every aspect of life. It is an undeniable leaning toward service that cannot be repressed. Paul says of his calling, "Woe is me if I do not preach the gospel!" (I Cor. 9:16). A servant's heart says, "Woe to me if I do not serve."

Therefore, a servant's heart is necessary. It is as necessary in God's economy as repentance, faith, water baptism or the in-filling of the Holy Spirit. The servanthood of the believer is a required step in the total salvation process. To deliberately reject a servant's heart in the time when its truth is revealed by the Holy Spirit is to disdain continuance in salvation (and continuance in salvation is the progressive embracing of Christ's lordship).

Granted then, that a servant's heart is required, how is it to be received? To answer, five thoughts should be considered. The first two points deal with what we may receive directly from God. The final three concern our response to Him in a way that expands a heart to serve in us.

1. To receive a servant's heart, become circumcised in heart. I believe that receiving a circumcised heart is crucial to servanthood. Circumcision of heart is a spiritual operation or surgery performed on the believer by God, available at salvation. It is not symbolic, but a real and essential spiritual experience. It is not a modern invention, but evident throughout the history of the Church, particularly in the Wesleyan tradition. Often it is called "holiness," "sanctification" or "entire sanctification."

> *In Him you were also circumcised with the circumcision made without hands, by putting off the body of the sins of the flesh, by the circumcision of Christ, buried with Him in baptism, in which you also were raised with Him through faith in the working of God, who raised Him from the dead.*
>
> Colossians 2:11-12

As natural circumcision was the commanded initiatory rite of Israel, as the sign of their covenant loyalty to God, so circumcision of the heart is now the necessary rite of New Covenant allegiance to Christ. Since servanthood and personal allegiance to Jesus are identical, how are Christians to be fully capable of serving without a circumcised heart? It is a God-promised provision to enable Christians to love or serve the Lord with all the heart and soul (Deut. 30:6).

The circumcision of the heart is an operation of removal. Christianity is not supposed to be an internal struggle between two natures, that takes place until death. Heart circumcision renders powerless and wholly eradicates the old nature. In physical circumcision the natural foreskin is removed. In spiritual circumcision the old stony heart is taken out and cast off. It is a dramatic and instantaneous cutting away of the sin nature, the complete separation of sin from the sinner.

The circumcision of the heart is also an operation of replacement, or transplant. In place of the former heart of stone, God gives a new heart of flesh. The believer receives a new nature that is eager, hungry, zealous and ready to receive God and all He has. He stands as a new creature with a clear conscience and is soft, tender in spirit and sensitive to the Holy Spirit and to others.

Natural circumcision leaves a physical mark on the body of the circumcised. Heart circumcision leaves the marks of servanthood on the spiritual body of the believer. We have already shown that the "marks of the Lord Jesus" professed by Paul were the results of his labors of service on behalf of the Church.

In order to receive and be established in the experience of a circumcised heart, you should first be convinced of its truth, that it is something that God has for you. As with the forgiveness of sins, the in-filling of the Spirit, healing, etc., circumcision of the heart is to be received in obedient, expectant faith. Thereafter you can truly present yourself to your Master, the Lord Christ, as His own captive love-slave, and you can present your body members as obedient instruments for the Lord's use alone (Rom. 6:4, 11, 13, 16).

2. To receive a servant's heart, participate in the servanthood sacrament of footwashing. "Sacrament" comes from a Latin term that means "an oath of allegiance, a consecration, a solemn obligation, or a holy act." A sacrament involves a physical action in obedience to the Lord, which then releases a spiritual transaction by a supernatural work of God. Sacraments take place corporately, within the context of the local church, and therefore the spiritual transaction that occurs is between God and man and between man and man. Every participation in a sacrament should result in the experience of grace and life from God, and in many cases, the sharing of grace and life between individuals.

The most widespread sacraments are water baptism and the Eucharist, or holy communion. There are other sacraments as well. The sacrament of footwashing is practiced in a number of Christian traditions.

Footwashing is an ordinance in which believers wash each other's feet. Of great importance is the fact that Christ instituted it in order to release servants' hearts in His disciples. At the Last Supper, Christ commanded His followers to continue the sacrament.

So when He had washed their feet, taken His garments, and sat down again, He said to them, "Do you know what I have done to you? You call me Teacher and Lord, and you say well, for so I am. If I then, your Lord and Teacher, have washed your feet, you also ought to wash one another's feet. For I have given you an example, that you should do as I have done to you. Most assuredly, I say to you, a servant is not greater than his master; nor is he who is sent greater than he who sent him. If you know these things, blessed are you if you do them."

John 13:12-17

Jesus washed the feet of His disciples first because at that time He was the only person present with a true servant's heart. He was so free and secure in His own identity that He did not fear losing status among His twelve servants.

A second purpose of footwashing is to remove enmity between Christian brethren, so that the second law of love may be fulfilled, "You shall love your neighbor as your-self" (Lev. 19:18). Participation in footwashing so releases a spirit of servanthood, that by it Christians can love and serve one another. Former ill feelings are cast aside, and relationships in Christ are more solidly cemented.

Footwashing also presents an opportunity for mutual refreshing among believers. Bare feet, even those with shoes, get dirty. They collect the dust of the world. In the same way souls become "soiled" from walking through the world, that is, in daily living. The issue is not the stain of sin, but the feeling of heaviness, discouragement or un-happiness that results from having resisted the world and its sin. Footwashing is among the ways that bring about refreshing. It is for the washing away of heaviness and the lifting of spirits. It is for knitting brethren together in spirit and soul and for demonstrating humility in service and love.

Thus footwashing is to be observed when sin or en-mity has separated brethren, when refreshing from the world is needed or for simply releasing servants' hearts in those who participate.

As in the case of all sacraments, the practice of foot-washing should be under proper leadership and in the context of the local church. In order to experience the sacrament of footwashing, you should follow the pattern of Jesus, using a basin of water and a towel. If necessary, begin by repenting from any attitude of pride, enmity, su-periority or desire to rule over others. Then receive the one who is washing your feet as though he were Jesus. When you, in turn, wash his or another's feet, you are to regard that person as the Lord. "Inasmuch as you did it to one of the least of these My brethren, you did it to Me" (Matt. 15:40).

Because it is a sacrament, grace and life are transacted between Christ and all participants. Genuine change takes place within. When you are doing the washing, you humble yourself and assume a servant's role. When you are being washed, you receive the sacrament by praying for the other. Both you and your fellow participants are blessed, and a servant's heart is indeed released in a greater measure in all.

3. To receive a servant's heart, spend time with Jesus, who is Servant of all. Receiving a servant's heart takes place secretly before the Lord. *Daily intimate communion with Jesus is vital.* You are to know Him through prayer, worship and listening. You are to let Jesus know you by sharing the deepest matters of your soul. When you dwell in the secret place of the Most High, you can then say, "I would rather be a doorkeeper—the lowliest servant—in the house of my God, if only to be near Him. As a deer to the pleasant streams, my soul pants and thirsts for intimate communion with my Lord. My very being aches with longings for Him" (see Psalm 84:10 and 42:1).

Jesus is our example. He received His servant's heart from the presence of His Father. At age twelve He asked, "Did you not know that I must be about My Father's business?" (Luke 2:49), and at age thirty-three He testified, "I always do those things that please Him" (John 8:29). In order to be attentive about His Father's business and to do all things so to please Him, Jesus spent time with His Father.

And when He had sent the multitudes away, He went up on the mountain by Himself to pray. Now when evening came, He was alone there.

Matthew 14:23

Now in the morning, having risen a long while before daylight, He went out and departed to a solitary place; and there He prayed.

Mark 1:35

When a servant's heart is developed in secret, its fruits may be recognized openly in the local church. Intimate communion keeps a person fresh and alive. He is made tender, touchable, sensitive and caring because of the Lord's touch upon his soul. The spirit he receives in private prayer is what he then communicates to others. When serving ceases, and especially when the spirit of serving has departed from an individual, it is evident that he no longer is loving his Jesus in secret.

4 To receive a servant's heart, be mentored by a servant. To receive the heart of a servant, you must follow one who is himself a servant, who himself has a servant's heart. Only one who has witnessed a thing through personal experience can then assist others to see from his point of view or lead them to the same experience. Only a true servant can lead another to genuine servanthood. "We speak what We know and testify what We have seen," Jesus said to Nicodemus (John 3:11). Because He witnessed the veracity of His own experience—what He knew and what He had seen—He led this inquiring Pharisee to know the same.

I urge you, brethren—you know the household of Stephanas, that it is the firstfruits of Achaia, and that

151

they have devoted themselves to the ministry of the saints—that you also submit to such, and to everyone who works and labors with us.

I Corinthians 16:15-16

To receive a servant's heart, look for a house like that of Stephanas. Find a household, a local church knit together in a close serving community.

Find the Stephanas who is head of that house. "Stephanas" means "crown." Find a pastor whose joy and crown is serving a people.

For what is our hope, or joy, or crown of rejoicing? Is it not even you in the presence of our Lord Jesus Christ at His coming? For you are our glory and joy.

I Thessaloninas 2:19-20

Find those who are devoted or "addicted" to service. "Addicted" means "consecrated, habituated or compulsively given." "Addicted" means "to be in bondage." Find those in bondage to serve, those who are bondslaves and love-slaves for Christ, those who are miserable unless they are serving.

The Scriptures command submission to such a serving people. Be joined to a serving church, then learn from everyone who is an addict to service. They are your mentors. They have been and are being mentored themselves.

To receive the heart of a servant involves both a spiritual experience and a learning process. "You must be born again," Christ commands (John 3:7). But newly born believers do not descend from the spiritual birth canal as sparkling, perfected servants. Servanthood, and the heart to serve, is both taught and received through mentoring of the local church. This is a lifelong process.

5. To receive a servant's heart, participate in service. "By reason of use" or practice, senses and skills are drilled and developed (Heb. 5:14). Practice serving to become skilled. Find all the service opportunities you can. As you serve, exercise faith. Believe that every act of serving causes you to receive more of His heart and more of His power.

Of these five reasons to serve, the very first is that practiced service might develop a servant's heart. Service that is regularly practiced yields other benefits as well: close interpersonal relationships are developed, leadership potential can be recognized and developed and natural and spiritual skills can be trained. The very last reason for serving that we teach is to get the job done.

Servanthood is a matter of opportunity, not oppression. Where there is no heart for service, no amount of teaching, training, urging or compelling will suffice. It is always a "have-to," not a "get-to." The so-called believer is a complainer. He sees himself as a victim of one service request after another. In his perspective, freedom and happiness would result from self-determination, from not being told what to do.

Excuses for not serving are also common. "I do not need to be a servant. That is a matter for full-time Christians. Besides, I can never begin to approach the servanthood of Christ. How could I? He was perfect. He was God. No, perfection is not for me in this life. I have tried and I cannot do it. He will perfect me in heaven, I am sure. In heaven there will be service enough."

The fact is, there is no such service in heaven. Tears are dried from every eye. There is no more crying, sorrow or pain. Earth is where service is needed, not heaven. Service is needed here, now.

When the change takes place on the inside through acquisition of a true heart of service, the matter of oppression is settled and all such excuse-making disappears.

In the servant's eyes, there is only opportunity. He is always watching for a new way to give. The influence of the servant's heart within him even brings about an occasional need to restrain from serving, just as Moses at a certain time had to restrain his people from giving any more to the Lord (Exod. 36:5-6).

The truth shall make you free (John 8:32). The truth that you can truly receive a servant's heart shall make you free. But how? Only if you as a disciple put the truth into practice. Truth makes free when it is obeyed by faith. You must believe and receive. *The Activated Church* can be either an oppressive threat or a delightful promise. Only you can decide which it will be for you.

Further Study for Personal Enrichment

Chapter Eight

1. What is a servant's heart?

2. Explain, in a paragraph, the importance of circumcision of the heart in your receiving a servant's heart.

3. Why should you follow Jesus' example in footwashing to fully appreciate the servant's heart with which God has blessed you? Answer in a paragraph.

4. Express why daily intimate communion with Jesus is vital for receiving a servant's heart.

5. If you have a mentor, write a thank-you note to him or her expressing your appreciation for your mentor's involvement in your life. If you do not have a mentor, write a prayer to God asking Him to provide you with one so your servant's heart may be fully developed.

6. In a day when addiction has such a negative meaning, express, in a brief paragraph, the importance of being positively addicted to service.

Further Study for Personal Enrichment
CONCLUDING QUESTION

In this book, *The Activated Church,* many profound and life-changing perspectives have been shared. Reflect upon what you have read; evaluate and express which truths impacted you the most. And, in a page, formulate a list of things you need to personally do to fulfill your mandate to be a servant in the activated Church.

> *...the throne of God and of the Lamb shall be in it, and His servants* [Greek: *douloi;* bondservants] *shall serve Him.*
>
> Revelation 22:3

Appendix

NOTE: The following charts and examples are to be used as models on how to structure and implement a servanthood program in a local church. Most of the examples are taken from the Custodial Crew Manual that is used in my church. However, this Appendix consists only of examples and is not a reproduction of the entire service manual.

Example of Overall Church Structure

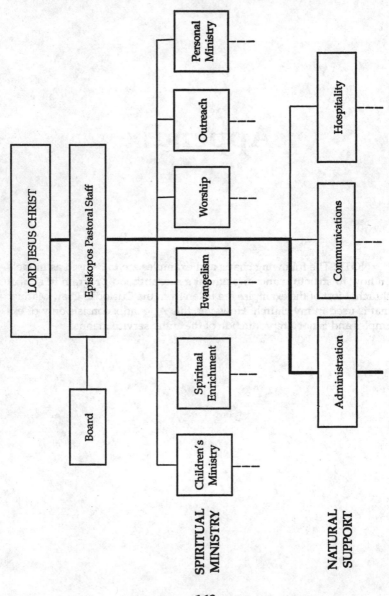

Example of a Specific Crew (Custodial) as Traced through the Administration Department of a Local Church

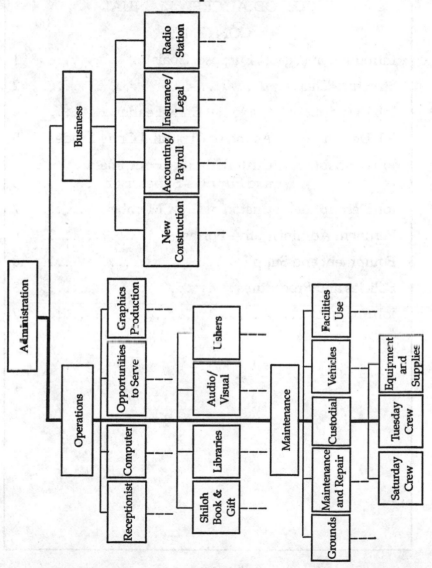

Example of Service Crew Manual Contents

CUSTODIAL CREW MANUAL

CONTENTS

Example of Service Crew Manual Job Description

JOB DESCRIPTION
CUSTODIAL CREW LEADER

The Custodial Crew Leader must have a close personal relationship with our Lord Jesus Christ and a God-given desire to serve Jesus and His Body. He is to be a challenging example to the crew members as expressed by:

1. A consistency with the vision of this local church.

2. His service and loyalty to the church.

3. His support of and service to the Custodial Crew members.

The purpose of the Living Faith Fellowship Custodial Crews is to minister to the Lord Jesus Christ by maintaining thorough cleanliness of the church building, developing a servant's heart within each crew member and nurturing close, interpersonal relationships between crew members. The impartation of this purpose is the responsibility of the Custodial Crew Leader. He is also responsible for the efficient operation of the Custodial Crew and the well-being of its members during the time of their service. Furthermore, to insure the efficient operation of the crew, it is the responsibility of the Custodial Crew Leader to invest the necessary time in planning and in preparation outside of the weekly scheduled crew sessions.

Other responsibilities include:

1. To prayerfully support the Custodial Crew.

2. To closely cooperate with the Building Maintenance Supervisor.

3. To write monthly reports for the Building Maintenance Supervisor.

4. To write bi-monthly evaluations of crew members for the Building Maintenance Supervisor.

5. To know all Custodial Crew policies, procedures and duties.

6. To insure that the Custodial Crew has all the necessary equipment and supplies on hand for each crew session.

7. To ensure that all tools and equipment are well maintained and in order.

8. To keep all records pertaining to the functions of Custodial Crew. These include attendance, assignments, purchases, inventories, projects, maintenance and reports.

9. To honestly communicate with his oversight if he is having any problems in this service.

Appendix

Example of a Service Evaluation for Crew Members

Evaluation of _____ Evaluated by _____

Area of Service_____ Date (of Evaluation) _____

Date (of Service) _____ Home Care Leaders _____

1. Attitude _____
_____
_____
_____
_____

2. Cooperation _____
_____
_____
_____
_____

3. Faithfulness _____ (Attendance Quotient:_____)
_____
_____
_____
_____

4. Quality Work _____
_____
_____
_____
_____

5. Developing a Sense_____
of Responsibility_____
_____
_____
_____

Example of a Service Evaluation for Supervisors

Evaluation of _____ Evaluated by _____

Area of Service _____ Date (of Evaluation) _____

Date (of Service) _____ Home Care Leaders_____

Supervisory Quality	Subjective Thoughts	Objective Rating
1. **Shepherd's Heart**—cares for sheep, gentleness, compassion, love; encourages, invests in, and develops sheep; watches out for their needs; people/relationship oriented; touchable		Outstanding
		Exceeds Expectations
		Satisfactory
		Needs Improvement
		Unsatisfactory
2. **Communication Skills**—over-communicates, gives and receives clear instruction, is easy to understand; report writing is clear and complete; maintains good contact with oversight and with crew, provides feedback, checks back with oversight		Outstanding
		Exceeds Expectations
		Satisfactory
		Needs Improvement
		Unsatisfactory
3. **Leadership Qualities**—teachable, servant's heart, leads rather than drives, servant of all vs. lording it over; ability to inspire and motivate, and impart vision, energy, and excitement; is a hard worker, serves as an example to others, knows how to ask for help when needed		Outstanding
		Exceeds Expectations
		Satisfactory
		Needs Improvement
		Unsatisfactory
4. **Administrative Skills**—coordination of people, coordination of projects; delegation; proper follow-up on delegated tasks and responsibilities; reports back to supervisor on progress and current status of projects, able to carry out another's vision, doesn't do his/her own thing		Outstanding
		Exceeds Expectations
		Satisfactory
		Needs Improvement
		Unsatisfactory

Supervisory Quality	Subjective Thoughts	Objective Rating
5. **Decision-Making Ability**—ability to think on feet, uses good judgment; knows how to think an issue through, thorough; can act quickly when under pressure; problem solving skills, knows when to check back, thinks like oversight		Outstanding
		Exceeds Expectations
		Satisfactory
		Needs Improvement
		Unsatisfactory
6. **Level of Initiative**—self starter, idea generator, follow through, energy and excitement Possible Levels: a) sees need, reports to oversight, then acts b) asks what to do c) waits until told what to do d) must be found in order to be told what to do		Outstanding
		Exceeds Expectations
		Satisfactory
		Needs Improvement
		Unsatisfactory
7. **Productivity**—a mind to work, hustle, intensity, accomplishes much, efficient, completes projects by assigned due dates, organized; uses good time management, able to motivate and coordinate others to accomplish goals		Outstanding
		Exceeds Expectations
		Satisfactory
		Needs Improvement
		Unsatisfactory
8. **Other (Optional)**		Outstanding
		Exceeds Expectations
		Satisfactory
		Needs Improvement
		Unsatisfactory

Definitions of Objective Rating Categories

OUTSTANDING (EXCELLENT)—has exceeded all expectations for this supervisory quality, and has made many significant contributions toward implementing Pastor's vision in this area.

EXCEEDS EXPECTATIONS—regularly works beyond a majority of expectations for this supervisory quality, and has made significant contributions toward implementing Pastor's vision.

SATISFACTORY—has met expectations for this supervisory quality and has contributed toward implementing Pastor's vision.

NEEDS IMPROVEMENT—has failed to meet minimum expectations for one or more of the significant aspects of this supervisory quality.

UNSATISFACTORY—has consistently failed to meet minimum expectations for this area of supervision.

ADDITIONAL MATERIALS, FURTHER STUDIES

To Pastors and Leaders

At Living Faith Fellowship, our burden is to help shepherds feed and tend their flocks and to build solid, healthy sheep. We are concerned with fulfilling the mandate to establish believers solidly in their faith and to enlarge the Kingdom of God through solid local churches.

We devote much time and many resources to provide local pastors with tools that work toward this end. By conviction, we share many of these tools with only Senior Pastors rather than to the mass market. As a result, the individual cost per unit of materials makes them best for those who are serious about using them.

We have produced materials for in-house use which are in continual revision and are, therefore, not published and sitting in inventory. However, we make them available to pastors and leaders who call or write for further information. Though this procedure may not be cost-effective for book publishing, we hold to this method by conviction in order to bless and build up the Body of Christ. We welcome you to contact us about our materials. In some cases, introductory lesson packets are available. We desire to serve and assist you in your ministry.

To Individuals

If you want to continue in further studies for personal enrichment which have subjective questions such as those in *The Activated Church*, simply contact Living Faith Fellowship for more information. We are dedicated to helping those who hunger for further growth in Jesus Christ.

Living Faith Fellowship
Ministry Training Center

Come and See Program

"What do I do now?"
"Where do I go from here?"
"Come and see for yourself!"

If you are a pastor or church leader and desire further help and assistance in implementing the vision described in this book, we have developed a "Come and See" program to aid and assist you.

Twenty years of growing, successful ministry have made Living Faith Fellowship Ministry Training Center a proven, solid, consistent leader in excellence and fruitful service. We want to serve the Body of Christ by helping build leaders who help Christ build His Church.

You can receive practical training and input by coming and seeing our church in action and meeting with our staff. There are many ideas floating around the Body of Christ today, but our heart is to offer practical assistance, not just give more ideas. We offer specific practical assistance in such areas as:

- **Worship**
- **Evangelism & Outreach**
- **Shepherding**
- **Spiritual Enrichment**
- **Children's Ministry**
- **Missions**
- **Hospitality**
- **Administration**
- **Public Relations**

If you desire further information on our "Come and See" program, it will be our delight to respond to your request. Please call or write:

**Living Faith Fellowship
Ministry Training Center
SW 345 Kimball
Pullman, WA 99163
(509) 332-3545**